IMAGINATION, UNDERSTANDING, AND THE VIRTUE OF LIBERALITY

IMAGINATION, UNDERSTANDING, AND THE VIRTUE OF LIBERALITY

by
David L. Norton

ROWMAN & LITTLEFIELD PUBLISHERS, INC.

ROWMAN & LITTLEFIELD PUBLISHERS, INC.

Published in the United States of America
by Rowman & Littlefield Publishers, Inc.
4720 Boston Way, Lanham, Maryland 20706

3 Henrietta Street
London WC2E 8LU, England

British Cataloging in Publication Information Available

Library of Congress Cataloging-in-Publication Data

Norton, David L.
Imagination, understanding, and the virtue of liberality / by
David L. Norton.
p.   cm.
Includes bibliographical references and index.
1. Toleration.   2. Empathy.   3. Imagination (Philosophy)
I. Title.
BJ1431.N67   1996   179'.9—dc20   95-38510   CIP

ISBN 0-8476-8127-0 (cloth: alk. paper)
ISBN 0-8476-8128-9 (pbk.: alk. paper)

Printed in the United States of America

 TM The paper used in this publication meets the minimum requirements of
American National Standard for Information Sciences—Permanence of
Paper for Printed Library Materials, ANSI Z39.48—1984.

To Daisaku Ikeda

There can be no value greater than the dignity of life,
and any attempt, whether religious or social,
to rate something higher must ultimately bring
oppression to humanity.
—Daisaku Ikeda

CONTENTS

PREFACE

This book is the continuation of a project that I began in 1976 with the publication of *Personal Destinies* and carried further in 1991 with *Democracy and Moral Development*.[1] In the first of these works I addressed the fundamental moral question, What is a worthy life for a human being? The second focused on the inescapable correlative, What is a good society? The answer and definition of a good society is a society whose institutions maximize the opportunity for worthy living among its constituents. Ex hypothesi, there will be theoretically an irreducible (but not unlimited) plurality of good societies, just as the answer to the question What is a worthy life? is pluralized by the individuation of persons.

In this book I do two things. I expand the horizon of my project to ask what kind of world can productively accommodate a plurality of good societies? I also identify some of the character traits that are required of individuals in order to sustain a productive, multicultural world, and the place within it of their own societies and their own lives. Foremost among these traits is the virtue of "liberality," the readiness to affirm truth and value in systems of belief and patterns of conduct different from one's own. The acquisition of this virtue is dependent upon the exercise by humans of the imaginative capacity to lend themselves to the alternative viewpoints of others. In the case of true (incommensurable) alternatives, this can occur only by substitution, which is to say, by temporarily setting aside one's accustomed perspective and adopting the other person's. This imaginative capacity is latent in all human beings, I believe, but needs to be made manifest if it is to be available for use. If the virtue of liberality has historically been rare among human beings, this may be attributable to a persistent historical underestimation (with a few notable exceptions) of the importance of imagination to knowledge and understanding—especially understanding of the self and of other persons. A consequence has been relative neglect, by dominant patterns of education, of the responsibility to nurture in young people the capacity for what Martin Buber termed "imagining the real."

Four persons have had a formative influence upon the thinking that appears in this book. Each is a living embodiment of the virtue of liberality. I am indebted first of all to Daisaku Ikeda for the lifetime that he has devoted to the promotion and cultivation of "world citizenship" in individuals and nations. Second, Tsunesaburo Makiguchi has sensitized me to the truth that the child is parent to the man (and correspondingly, the woman). Third, Michael Krausz has lent his critical acumen to every page and every line of several manuscript drafts in order that this book might say more effectively what I intended. A few words about these three are in order.

At age nineteen, in war-ravaged Japan, Daisaku Ikeda consecrated his life to peace. In his rise from humble origins to the presidency of the Soka Gakkai (Society for Values-Creation), a lay Buddhist organization with more than eleven million members in Japan and 115 other countries, and thereafter to the presidency of Soka Gakkai International, he has adhered unwaveringly to this ideal. Step by step he has acquired the practical resourcefulness and the personal virtues that have enabled him to work continuously and effectively toward this ideal with political and intellectual leaders of the world. In Japan, he and the Soka Gakkai have resolutely lent their strength to the processes of democratization that began with the American occupation after World War II. They have steadfastly opposed reactionary initiatives toward the reestablishment of au-

thoritarian government whose strategy has been to stigmatize democratic gains as "the excesses of democracy." The thriving institutions
Ikeda has founded in Japan, notable among them the Soka Education System, the Min-On Concert Association, the Tokyo Fuji Art
Museum, and a publications conglomerate whose centerpiece is the
newspaper *Seikyo Shimbun*, circulation 5,500,000, have assiduously
promoted cultural exchange in the interest of cross-cultural understanding. In this same interest, Ikeda was the first Japanese leader to
initiate dialogue with leaders in the former USSR and China toward
restoring amicable relations between these countries and Japan. For
many years his "citizen diplomacy" has been directed toward limited world federation through a restructured United Nations. In 1983
he was the recipient of the United Nations Peace Award.

At the same time he has with equal energy and practical wisdom
promoted what he calls a human revolution aimed at transforming
the consciousnesses of individual human beings in order to sustain
peace and productivity in an interactive multicultural world of the
twenty-first century. His emphases upon "soft power" and "inner
motivation" express the pantheistic Buddhist understanding that the
sacred is not above and beyond the natural world but within every
human being; and it is the responsibility of individuals and societies
alike to support discovery and manifestation of the divine in and by
all persons. Because its manifestation takes different forms in different persons and different cultures, this Buddhist conception is inherently pluralistic, and the harmonization of diversity becomes the
foremost social and political challenge.

The harmonization of diversity is remarkably exemplified in Ikeda
himself, by the prismatic perception with which he seeks out and
affirms multifarious virtues in far-flung cultures and disparate persons. Indicative of this is the presence in the vestibule of Ikeda Auditorium at Soka University, Tokyo, of massive statues of Victor Hugo,
Leo Tolstoy, and Walt Whitman. At one level they symbolize the contributions of their cultures to the heritage of humankind; at a second
level the three figures represent the genius, or Buddha Nature, that
exists innately, not just in such culture heroes as Hugo, Tolstoy, and
Whitman but also within every human being. At yet another level
their presence in the auditorium expresses the Buddhist teaching

that in the interest of spiritual health, ethnocentrism, like egoism, must be overcome not by abandoning local loyalties but by (in Plato's words) "being of another mind" in maintaining them. The content of the present book then is offered as a contribution to Ikeda's conceptualization of the human revolution that productive living in the situation of cooperative diversity will require.

Tsunesaburo Makiguchi was a dedicated Japanese teacher and educational reformer until, in 1932, the militarized Japanese government forbade him these activities. He became the founder and first president of the Soka Gakkai, and died in a Japanese prison in 1944, after being confined for refusing to compromise his own Buddhist beliefs and practices and those of the Soka Gakkai in accordance with the mandated national religion of Shinto. The fundamental aim of Makiguchi's proposed educational reforms was to preserve and strengthen in children and young people their inborn motivation to learn and to grow, the original manifestation of the "inner motivation" by which one's innate potential worth, or Buddha Nature, is progressively actualized. To this end, he proposed that the aim of education must be the happiness of children now, and not a happiness projected for later life. By "happiness" Makiguchi referred not to pleasure but to the satisfaction of work well done when it is the right work for the individual to do. Children's primary work is learning, and they experience happiness at it provided that parents and teachers respect their spontaneous interests. Their spontaneous interests can be shaped, channeled, focused, and redirected; but when these interests are declared irrelevant in favor of an adult-imposed curriculum, inner motivation to learn is supplanted in education by external motivators such as grades, diplomas, and adult approval that is attendant upon these. This prolonged conditioning in working for external rewards produces adults who recognize no other motivation and predictably perpetuate the pattern in which they were reared. The result is that their distinctive innate potential worth goes unactualized; they will be vulnerable to corruption by the simple logic that corrupt practices typically promise greater extrinsic rewards.

What Makiguchi teaches is that the inner motivation upon which the best adult lives are lived must be respected and nurtured beginning in earliest childhood. Under the influence of his writings, to which I was introduced by Dr. Dayle M. Bethel of Kyoto, I undertook five years ago a program of extensive on-site studies of elementary and secondary classrooms in the United States and Japan. It has enduringly and profoundly reshaped my thinking about a question that has always preoccupied me, What constitutes good growth for human beings?

My indebtedness to Michael Krausz is on a more immediate level. He has read and criticized each of the following chapters in successive revisions, and such cogency as they possess is largely attributable to him. In our many sessions together, he persistently called my attention to needed clarifications and to faulty or missing argumentation; and he unerringly directed me to countertheses by others or by himself that my case obliged me to address. His sole purpose was to help me to improve both my understanding and my presentation of my own views, which in two or three important matters differ from his. (A reading of his *Rightness and Reasons* convincingly attests that Michael wants only his opponents' best case, and if they have presented something less, he will improve upon it for them.) For his unstinting generosity in lending his expertise to my work, I am more grateful than words can express.

Fourth and finally, it is my good fortune to live with an exceptionally keen-minded philosopher—my wife, Mary K. Norton. Our continuous dialogue on philosophical issues related to her work and to mine have immeasurably enriched my writings as they have enriched my life.

Note

1. *Personal Destinies* (Princeton, N.J.: Princeton University Press, 1976); *Democracy and Moral Development* (Berkeley: University of California Press, 1991).

ACKNOWLEDGMENTS

My husband, David L. Norton, died on July 24, 1995, after a brief battle with cancer that had been diagnosed only twelve days before. At the time it looked as if the publication of *Imagination, Understanding, and the Virtue of Liberality* would be the first casualty of his illness. But Dave's friend, Michael Krausz, immediately took up the task of placing the orphaned manuscript in the hands of a publisher. Thanks to his tireless efforts, the generous help of Eva Brann, and Jonathan Sisk's perceptive appreciation of the quality of the book, it was placed with Rowman & Littlefield. Michael called us at the hospital where Dave endured the last five days of his life to tell us that a contract was on the way. Dave, who by then spoke rarely, said, "Tell Michael I love him. He's a magician. He is the best."

Paul Durbin, one of Dave's colleagues in the Department of Philosophy of the University of Delaware and one of our oldest and dearest friends, has been nothing short of heroic in the help he has given me to prepare the manuscript of *Imagination, Understanding, and the Virtue of Liberality* for publication. He has shielded me from overwhelming details and difficulties; he has encouraged and supported me; and he has been by my side since the start of Dave's illness with a loyalty and steadfastness the like of which is found only in ancient *chansons de geste*. Both he and Michael Krausz combine an unequaled intellectual acuity with a rare generosity of spirit. Men such as they are what Aristotle must have meant by "great-souled men," and both profoundly enriched Dave's life as they do mine.

Gail Ross has been unstinting in her patient willingness to make corrections to Dave's manuscript, and I am immeasurably grateful for her constant professionalism.

In the desolation of my husband's death, I have been sustained by the love of our children, Anita Kronsberg and Ron, Peter, Tucker, and Cory Norton. They are such blessings: each radiates their father's spirit in a unique and delightful way.

I would like to add my voice to Dave's in dedicating this book to our Beloved Teacher Ikeda. It is he who first lifted our eyes to a broader horizon through our visits to Japan to meet with him and members of the Soka Gakkai, a worldwide community of people who exemplify the virtue of liberality.

Mary K. Norton

Chapter 1

TRANSCENDENTAL IMAGINATION AND ALTERNATIVE WORLDS

The "Transcendental" Function

E veryday discourse includes the phrase, "lending oneself to the viewpoint of another." It is not, I think, a mere figure of speech. My purposes are threefold: to show that this phrase refers to a genuine human capacity, to provide an explanation of this capacity in terms of the functional organization of human consciousness, and to demonstrate that the ability to call upon the capacity is indispensable to well-lived lives.

What we normally mean by "knowledge" of another person or people is an accounting of the way they appear to us, from our viewpoint. In contrast, when I refer to "understanding" others I mean a direct acquaintance with the way they and their worlds appear to them. By "the way they appear to us," I refer not to the bare facts of their appearance but to the meaning such facts have for us; and by "the way they and their worlds appear to them," I refer to the meaning for them of whatever their experience presents

1

to them, including themselves (and us, if we have appeared to them). To understand another person or people requires that we trade places with them by what Max Scheler called "participatory enactment" of their lives. This participatory enactment is not literal, it is imaginative; and it is this function of imagination that will be my subject throughout.

My leave to focus upon just one of the functions of imagination has been granted by the recent publication of Eva Brann's comprehensive study of all of the functions that have been attributed to the imagination in the history of Western thought.[1] But while my focus is narrow in the context of that history, it is, so to speak, a portal that opens upon limitless vistas that are alluded to in the well-known musing of William James: "Normal human consciousness is only a narrow extract from a great sea of possible human consciousness."[2]

James was referring to other consciousnesses to which the effects of nitrous oxide appeared to afford access. The "other consciousness" with which I am concerned is the perspectival worlds of other persons, beginning with persons whose basic beliefs and patterns of conduct differ strikingly from our own. My thesis is that our access to these perspectival worlds is afforded by imagination, which I here define in preliminary fashion as the faculty that apprehends possibilities.

In a digest of Western thought on the functions of imagination, John Kekes identifies four that are "particularly important."

> The first is the formation of images, like the face of an absent friend; the second is resourceful problem solving, exemplified, for instance, by nonlinear thinking; the third is the falsification of some aspect of reality, as when we fantasize that the facts are other than they are; and the fourth is the mental exploration of what it would be like to realize particular possibilities, such as being very rich.[3]

I am confining my discussion to this fourth category. My intent is to show that it is an essential but neglected dimension of well-lived lives.

I will speak of the perspectival world a person or a people presently inhabit as their "actual" world. Every actual world contains innumerable possibilities that its inhabitants continually canvas in order to prepare themselves for what the future may demand of them. This is an adaptive function, and it is what first comes to mind when Abraham Maslow says, "Man has his future within him, dynamically active at this present moment."[4] Because the possibilities that we adaptively scan in this manner are continuous with actuality, I will call them "immanent possibilities." Proponents of what Arthur O. Lovejoy named the "principle of plenitude," from Aristotle to Nelson Goodman, hold that all possibilities are implicit in what is actual.[5] I think this is incorrect for the following reason: what makes an actual world a world is that the viewpoint that organizes it is capable of assimilating everything that may be presented to it by actual or possible experience. But this "closure" excludes everything that experience may present in the different aspects that are disclosed by alternative perspectives. These excluded aspects I will call "transcendental possibilities" in relation to the world that excludes them.

The best account of the capacity of a viewpoint to encompass whatever experience has brought or may bring (closure) is by C. I. Lewis, for whom the heart of a viewpoint is a set of categories of perception and cognition. In Lewis's words,

> The principles of categorical interpretation are a priori valid of all possible experience because such principles express the criteria of the veridical and the real. . . . If it be asked . . . "How do we know . . . that we may not be presented in experience with what will not fit into any category and thus be wholly unintelligible," the answer is . . . What is not reality of one sort is reality of another; what we do not understand in one way, we shall understand in another. The subsumption of the given under the heading "dream" or "illusion" is itself a categorical interpretation by which we understand certain experiences. Even "the unintelligible" is a sort of category, a temporary pigeon-hole in which items are filed subject to later classification. . . . In determining its own interpretations—and only so—the mind legislates for reality, no matter what future experience may bring.[6]

From the comprehensiveness of every perspectival world, it follows that alternative perspectival worlds are closed off—

discontinuous—to one another. Because immanent possibilities are continuous with the existing world, they can be accessed by inference, generalization, and other extrapolative procedures; and the claims they make upon existing feeling and volition are additive and not transformative. However, transcendent possibilities cannot be thus accessed and encompassed, because by virtue of the closure of the existing world, they stand as discontinuous "beyonds."

I propose that such possibilities can be apprehended by the transcendental function of imagination. The central premise of my thesis was expressed by the Roman poet Terence: "Nihil humani a me alienum," which I here generalize as "Nothing human is alien to any of us."[7] To be a human being is to contain within oneself all human possibilities. Human beings differentiate themselves culturally and individually by actualizing different possibilities, but the possibilities that are actualized by other persons are within us as possibilities and are available for participatory enactment by transcendental imagination.

My intent in this introduction is to demonstrate the importance of transcendental imagination by means of examples, but first I must forestall some misunderstandings that might otherwise be fostered by my use of the word "transcendental." First, my meaning for the term has no relation to Kant's meaning in his *Critique of Pure Reason*. Kant there applies the term to what is beneath knowledge of the world in the sense of providing its a priori conditions, namely the a priori Forms of Sensibility and Categories of the Understanding that Kant claimed to arrive at by regressive analysis. It is worth adding that imagination as I present it in this book has nothing to do with the imagination that for Kant in *Critique of Pure Reason* is the interface between the Forms of Sensibility and the Categories of the Understanding. As did Descartes and Hume before him, Kant here employs imagination to plug a breach in his doctrine that the doctrine itself has created. I think we witness here a modern misdirection in the understanding of imagination that is partly responsible for our widespread present failure to recognize the vital importance of imagination's transcendental function, but to support this assertion here by the requisite detailed study in the history of ideas would be a distraction from our course.

4

From another quarter, Romanticism's "transcendental" is akin to mine in referring to what is "beyond" the everyday world and not "beneath" it as the set of epistemic preconditions of the way the world appears to us. However, Romanticism attributes to its "beyond" a metaphysical superiority that I in no way intend. According to Henri Bergson, for example, the transcendence afforded by "intuition" (this term is often used interchangeably with "imagination" in Romantic literature) serves "to brush aside the utilitarian symbols, the conventional and socially accepted generalities, in short, everything that veils reality from us, in order to bring us face to face with reality itself."[8] Romanticism's dualism is an advance upon the positivism of supposing the existing world to be the only world possible; but its claim to exchange it for perspectiveless and immediate reality is insupportable, for perspectiveless immediacy is, as Santayana has said, "incompatible with being alive," excluding as it does "any particular station, organ, interest, or date of survey."[9] Romanticism's usage parallels the "God's eye" meaning of "the transcendent" in dualistic religion, with which my meaning likewise does not correspond.

Finally, in the current epistemological debate between relativists and antirelativists, the term "transcendental" is often used to refer to perspective-free knowledge, that is, to knowledge that is unconditioned by the knower, the impossibility of which I (with leading disputants on both sides of the debate) take to have been established by Kant. I believe that transcendence lands us not in ultimate and perspectiveless reality, but in an alternative perspectival world, the elaboration of which falls to the faculties of "bound consciousness."[10]

A Dialectical Relationship

The dialectical relationship between transcendental imagination and what I call "bound consciousness"—comprising faculties that are bound to the progressive elaboration of a continuum—was described by Plato in the *Ion* and the *Timaeus*. In the *Timaeus* he says, "No man, when in his wits, attains prophetic truth and inspiration." To receive the "inspired word" it is necessary that one's intelligence "be enthralled." Plato hastens to add that once the illumination has appeared, a person must "first recover his wits" if he "would understand what he remembers to have been said . . . or would determine by reason the meaning of the apparitions which he has seen."[11] A dialectic that is in important respects comparable to Plato's is to be found in Kant's *Critique of Judgment*—historically a bridge between the Enlightenment and Romanticism—as the interplay between "genius" (Plato's "inspiration") and "talent" (Plato's "wits"). To collect the antecedents to what I call "transcendental imagination" (Plato, the Kant of the *Critique of Judgment*, the Romantics, and Giambattista Vico would have a central place) is an attractive prospect, but once again the history of ideas would be a distraction here.

What is the point of troubling to exchange perspectives upon the world and ourselves when the new perspective is not inherently superior to the old? The point is to arrive at understanding of other peoples and persons, as well as of ourselves. What we ordinarily mean by knowledge of other persons is the meaning they have for us, in our perspective. In contrast, my meaning of understanding another requires us to perceive the world and the other in his or her perspective. Reflexively, this provides the differentiae without which we cannot know ourselves as individuals, that is, as each a distinctive one among others of our kind. The requisite knowledge of others can be called "internal" as distinguished from "external," and it is internal knowledge for which I employ the word "understanding."

To demonstrate the importance of transcendental imagination, I will draw upon the testimony of specialists in several fields of inquiry who show that successful practice in their fields is dependent upon the employment of this faculty. The fields are cultural anthropology, history, ethics, social philosophy, education, and developmental psychology. The respective spokesmen are Clifford Geertz, R. G. Collingwood, R. M. Hare, Max Scheler and Martin Buber, Bertand Russell and Hare again. In developmental psychology, I will supply a list of contemporary theorists when I discuss the topic.

Imagination in Cultural Anthropology: Clifford Geertz

According to Geertz, understanding the people of another culture depends upon achieving an "actor-oriented" interpretation of their

6

beliefs and conduct, which is to say the people's own understanding.[12] Emphasizing that this requires an "imaginative act," he compares it to the way both author and readers of a novel enter into the lives of its *dramatis personae*.[13] Tightening the analogy, he identifies anthropological studies as "fictions,"

> fictions in the sense that they are "something made," "something fashioned"—the original meaning of *fictio*—not that they are false, unfactual, or merely "as if" thought experiments. To construct the actor-oriented descriptions of the involvements of a Berber chieftain, a Jewish merchant, and a French soldier with one another in 1912 Morocco [an historical episode Geertz has earlier described and interpreted] is clearly an imaginative act, not all that different from constructing similar descriptions of, say, the involvements with one another of a provincial French doctor, his silly, adulterous wife, and her feckless lover in nineteenth century France. In the latter case, the actors are represented as not having existed and the events as not having happened, while in the former they are represented as actual, or as having been so. This is a difference of no mean importance; indeed, precisely the one Madame Bovary had difficulty grasping. But the importance does not lie in the fact that her story was created while Cohen's was only noted. The conditions of the creation, and the point of it (to say nothing of the manner and the quality) differ. But the one is as much a *fictio*—"a making"—as the other.[14]

Geertz calls ethnography a semiotic enterprise, which is to say that its data—the words, conduct, artifacts, and such, of the people under study—are signifiers of meanings that it is the work of ethnography to discern. The problem is that particular meanings are implicated in the "webs of significance" that constitute cultures.[15] If the ethnographer is to arrive at the meaning of her data for the people she is studying, she must exchange her own web of significance for theirs—an act of perspectival world-exchange that Geertz rightly attributes to the imagination.

Imagination in Historical Inquiry: R. G. Collingwood

Collingwood's theory of historical understanding as "imaginative re-enactment" is isomorphic with Geertz's account of cross-cultural understanding. The historian's task is to understand events of the past as they were understood by the people who participated in them. Collingwood says, "So the historian of politics or warfare, presented with an account of certain actions done by Julius Caesar, tries to understand these actions, that is, to discover what thoughts in Caesar's mind determined him to do them. This implies envisaging for himself what Caesar thought about the situation and the possible ways of dealing with it."[16] By my argument the historian and his or her readers are capable of doing this because within them are the possibilities that Caesar actualized.[17]

Like Geertz, Collingwood stresses that a historical study is a *fictio* in that (1) it is made by the historian, and (2) it is a work of imagination that in this respect resembles the construction of a novel. He notes the conventional supposition that the historian's work is "pegged down, so to speak, to the facts by statements of authorities, which we regard as data or fixed points for the work of the construction."[18] However, this misrepresents the situation because the data must themselves be interpreted by the historian and are thus outcomes and not antecedent givens. From his own work on Roman Britain, Collingwood provides the following illustration.

> Suetonius tells me that Nero at one time intended to evacuate Britain. I reject this statement, not because any better authority flatly contradicts it, for of course none does; but because my reconstruction of Nero's policy based on Tacitus will not allow me to think that Suetonius is right. And if I am told that this is merely to say I prefer Tacitus to Suetonius, I confess that I do; but I do so just because I find myself able to incorporate what Tacitus tells me into a coherent and continuous picture of my own, and cannot do this for Suetonius.[19]

The subjects of the historian's study inhabit a world of interconnected meanings, and the same is true of the historian and his or her readers. But they are alternative worlds, separated by a gulf of discontinuity that cannot be bridged by inference. For this reason Collingwood is correct in insisting that the historian's access is afforded by imagination.

> As works of imagination, the historian's and the novelist's do not differ. Where they do differ is that the historian's picture is meant to be true.

8

The novelist has a single task only; to construct a coherent picture, one that makes sense. The historian has a double task: he has both to do this, and to construct a picture of things as they really were and of events as they really happened. This further imposes upon him obedience to three rules of method, from which the novelist or artist is free.[20]

Collingwood proceeds to list and describe the three rules of historicist method, but our path now turns us to the case for the indispensability of transcendental imagination to the conduct of moral life as it is presented by R. M. Hare.

Imagination in Moral Life: R. M. Hare

Hare begins with the proposition that moral conduct depends upon our ability to put ourselves imaginatively in the places of others in order to judge the effects of our prospective conduct upon them. To do this we must imagine that we are in their circumstances, not as ourselves but as the others, for otherwise we cannot learn "what it is like for him."[21] Hare says, "I emphasize that the imagined situation must be one in which I have his preferences."[22]

Hare acknowledges the apparent paradox in imagining to be another when the other's preferences and situation are "so unlike those of myself and my present situation." The apparent paradox exists when "so unlike" implies incommensurability, because incommensurables cannot be coherently combined. Hare argues that the paradox is merely apparent, not real, because the imaginative act in question functions not additively but by substitution. "Putting myself in someone else's shoes does not involve supposing myself to have simultaneously two incompatible sets of properties; it involves . . . supposing that I might lose one set and acquire another."[23] The imaginative identity-exchange that Hare here invokes as a condition of moral life is a function of what I have termed "transcendental imagination." In my thesis, it is a human capacity because the personal properties that constitute the actuality of the other are within each of us as possibilities.

What must be noted in Hare's case concerning moral conduct is

9

that it applies to persons who share the same language system, and this is also true of the theses concerning interpersonal understanding by Martin Buber and Max Scheler to which we will turn next. Thanks to the "linguistic turn" of twentieth-century Anglo-American philosophy, the question of commensurability of perspectival worlds has become equated with the intertranslatability of expressions between language systems. That this is not the same issue is indicated in George Bernard Shaw's well-known observation that the English people and the American people are divided by their common language. Two people in alternative perspectival worlds may well use the same word, but in incommensurably different ways. Moreover, a demonstration that each can understand the other's meaning of the word is not a demonstration of commensurability, for incommensurability will obtain if each cannot accept the other's meaning without introducing transformative reverberations throughout his or her perspectival world. Correlatively, translatability between language does not demonstrate commensurability or understanding. We can and do translate *eros* as "love," *arete* as "virtue," and *eudaimonia* as "happiness"; but if we impose our meanings of the translated terms, they will block our access to the perspectival world of the Hellenes. Conversely, thanks to the polysemy of our language, translation can afford to us a sufficient measure of the Greek understanding of these terms to make it clear that acceptance of the Greek meanings entails abandonment of our familiar meanings, that is, it can only occur by substitution and not by adding their meanings to ours. In chapter 2, I will develop this as the idea that "incommensurable" is to be understood not as "untranslatable," but as "incompossible."

Imagination in Interpersonal Relations:
Martin Buber and Max Scheler

In Buber's and Scheler's analyses of interpersonal relations, the pivot is the previously mentioned distinction between "external" and "internal" knowledge of other persons. External knowledge discloses him or her in our perspective, while internal knowledge occurs by adoption of the other's perspectival world and discloses the world and the self of the other as they appear to him or her.

Describing internal knowledge, Buber says, "He is no longer He or She, limited by other Hes and Shes, a dot in the world grid of space and time, nor a condition that can be experienced and described, a loose bundle of named qualities. Neighborless and seamless, he is Thou and fills the firmament. Not as if there were nothing but he; but everything else lives in his light."[24] Calling internal knowledge "personal making present," Buber says,

> It rests on a capacity possessed to some extent by everyone, which may be described as "imagining" the real; I mean the capacity to hold before one's soul a reality arising at this moment but not able to be directly experienced. Applied to intercourse between men, "imagining" the real means that I imagine to myself what another man is at this very moment wishing, feeling, perceiving, thinking, and not as a detached content but in his very reality, that is, as a living process in this man.[25]

For Buber, to be a person is to be the organizing center and source of a world of interrelated meanings, and it is in this sense that the other as Thou "fills the firmament . . . [and] everything else lives in his light." Notice that Buber's expression "imagining the real" serves nicely to distinguish the *fictios* of cultural anthropology and of history from the *fictio* of the novelist, as that distinction is made by Geertz and Collingwood.

I think Buber's belief that the capacity for imagining the real is "possessed to some extent by everyone," at least as a "partial happening," is illustrated by the experience of seeing ourselves through the eyes of another. It is invariably a startling occurrence because of the disparity between the other's (external) view of us and our own. In chapter 3 I will undertake a phenomenological analysis of the shock that attends the exchange of discontinuous perspectives.

According to Max Scheler, internal knowledge of another is achieved by "participatory enactment." Of external knowledge Scheler says, "The values attaching to the physical, the corporal, and the mental can all be given to us objectively and may even be so given in the process of loving those who possess them. But this

11

does not apply to the purely personal values, i.e., the value of the personality itself. So long as we continue to "objectify" someone in this way, his personality eludes our grasp, and only the trappings remain." Turning to internal knowledge Scheler says, "The person of the other can only be disclosed by my joining in the performance of his acts, either cognitively, by 'understanding' and vicariously 're-living,' or morally, by 'following in his footsteps.' "[26] On the reflexive side, Scheler emphasizes that only by participatory enactment are we able "to effect a real *enlargement* of our own lives and to transcend the limitations of our actual experience."[27] Later we will elaborate upon this theme in terms of the inevitable parochialism of lives that do not undergo enlargement through the exercise of transcendental imagination.

For both Buber and Scheler, internal knowledge is direct acquaintance with the unique personhood of the other. In the words of Samuel Taylor Coleridge, "She, she herself and only She, shone in her body visibly."[28] This does not refer to perspectiveless knowledge of the other, but rather to knowledge of her in her own perspective, which I am terming understanding.

It is important to recognize that Scheler uses the term "cognitive" in the broad Cartesian sense, as inclusive of emotion, sensation, volition, memory, and imagination, as well as cognition. (There is a notable difference between Scheler and Collingwood: see note 17.) Scheler ascribes to imagination the agency in "vicarious re-living," but it does not act independently; imagination brings the other dimensions of subjectivity with it. By implication, Scheler is addressing the age-old question of the relationship of imagination and cognition (narrowly defined). He holds that it is not inherently adversarial, but complementary. This echoes the complementarity of "inspiration" and "wits" according to Plato, and of "genius" and "talent" according to Kant in the *Critique of Judgment*.

It must also be noted that Scheler's two ways of joining in the performance of another are not to be regarded as disjunctive. This is because "following in the footsteps" of another (the moral way) involves a radical disparity when the person one follows is not following in the footsteps of someone else. From this it is clear that Scheler's moral means must be attended by his cognitive means if internal knowledge of the other is to result. Conversely, modeling one's life on that of another is by no means a necessary condition for gaining internal knowledge of him or her. To employ a religious analogue, revelation is not conversion and need not be attended by conversion. But the analogy abruptly ends, because what revelation discloses in our case is not the divinity that provides salvation (a revelation from which conversion surely ought to follow) but the perspectival world of another person. Normally participatory enactment of the life of another is followed by resumption of one's life; its purpose is not to replicate the life of the other in actuality but to understand the other, and by that understanding to better live one's own life, including one's relations to others.

Imagination in Education: R. M. Hare and Bertrand Russell

The difference between external and internal knowledge of other persons is employed by Buber and Scheler to distinguish "the social" from "the interpersonal." I want now to make use of this distinction in order to show that an enterprise that by general agreement is paramount within the sphere of the social—namely education—is in fact dependent upon the interpersonal in the sense of interpersonal employed by Buber and Scheler. As it happens, Hare and Russell are both educators and philosophers who speak of learning within their discipline; but it will be readily apparent that what they say is applicable to learning in general.

R.M. Hare says, "Nothing is so difficult in philosophical writing as to get people to be sympathetic enough to what one is saying to understand what it is. Perhaps nobody will ever understand a philosophical book of any depth without, initially, believing it, or at least suspending his disbelief. Otherwise he will never grasp what the writer is intending to convey."[29] Notice the implicit distinction here between "knowing" what an author has said, and "understanding" it. A reader may claim to know what an author says, and demonstrate it—for example by repeating a given page verbatim—without in the least understanding it in Hare's meaning of that term.

Hare's wording echoes Coleridge's famous dictum that the adven-

13

ture of imagination requires "the willing suspension of disbelief."[30] It is a precondition of "lending" oneself to the viewpoint of another, as for example a reader lends herself to the viewpoint of the protagonist of a novel or to the viewpoint of the Ancient Mariner. Hare's indication that the same process is involved in learning from a work of philosophy receives independent corroboration from Bertrand Russell in a passage that deserves to be cited in full because of its force and eloquence.

> In studying a philosopher, the right attitude is neither reverence nor contempt, but first a kind of hypothetical sympathy, until it is possible to know what it feels like to believe in his theories, and only then a revival of the critical attitude, which should resemble, as far as possible, the state of mind of a person abandoning opinions which he has hitherto held. Contempt interferes with the first part of this process, and reverence with the second. Two things are to be remembered: that a man whose opinions and theories are worth studying may be presumed to have had some intelligence, but that no man is likely to have arrived at complete and final truth on any subject whatever. When an intelligent man expresses a view which seems to us obviously absurd, we should not attempt to prove that it is somehow true, but we should try to understand how it ever came to seem true. This exercise of historical and psychological imagination at once enlarges the scope of our thinking and helps us to realize how foolish many of our own cherished prejudices will seem to an age which has a different temper of mind.[31]

In an earlier citation, Max Scheler said that only by "participatory enactment" are we able "to effect a real *enlargement* of our own lives and to *transcend* the limitations of our actual experience." I take this to be an important point—the remarks of both Hare and Russell, as stated explicitly in Russell's closing sentence. Hare and Russell are saying that the exercise of what I call transcendental imagination is crucial to any learning that (in Russell's words) "enlarges the scope of our thinking." This leads me to propose that an education system is gravely deficient if it neglects the work of expressly cultivating transcendental imagination as I believe our established pattern of formal education in the United States does. In chapters 3 and 4 I will offer evidence of this neglect, together with

14

an analysis of its causes and some discussion of teaching strategies by which it can be rectified.

The "Common Ground" Approach to Commensuration

Regarding the intercultural and interpersonal understanding with which we have so far been concerned, what is to be said of the prevalent thesis that it can be achieved by means of shared characteristics—a contention that, if true, renders otiose the transcendental imagination we are investigating?

I will call shared characteristics "universals" and characteristics that distinguish peoples and persons from one another "variables." Then the mistake in the common-ground approach lies in treating universals and variables independently, when in fact universals contain variables as latent properties, and it is manifest variables that determine the meaning of the universals for the people whose variables they are.

Geertz shows that the common-ground (in his term, "consensus gentium") approach fails in cultural anthropology, because in order to preserve their universality, the universals must be emptied of all content. When, for example, Malinowski gives his candidate for universality—religion—even the minimal content of a "sense of Providence," this providence either cannot embrace alike Confucians, Zen Buddhists, Tibetan Buddhists, and scientific naturalists, or else it is made to embrace them by radically altering the meaning of a "sense of Providence" in each case, thereby destroying its universality.[32]

We will recognize that the bifurcation of universals and variables is an abstractionist fallacy if we notice, on one hand, that universal traits (we are born, we must eat and drink, we make dwellings and tools, we reproduce, we die) are too meager to add up to a human life. To be recognizably human, a life must include variables as well as universals, which is to say that variables and universals are interdependent. From the other end it is the particular variables that give universals the meaning they have for a particular people.

If we do not know the meaning that death has for a given people, the meaning that love has for them, and so on, we do not understand that people. It gets us nowhere to observe that, like all people, they are mortal, for example, when thanatology discloses immense variety in the meanings that the fact of their own mortality has for different peoples.

The reason that universals vary in their meaning for different peoples is that meaning derives from purpose, and purposes are variable. Meaning is significance, both in its sense of signification and in its sense of importance. To a creature without purpose nothing would signify, because attention would be dispersed and without focus—significance would be deprived of its selective function, which is to say it would not exist.

The same is the case for persons within a shared culture. Here it is not false to speak of shared beliefs, shared values, and shared customs; but to suppose that what is thus shared is identical in meaning is an abstractionist fallacy. Indeed, as social scientists and social philosophers have noted, it is precisely the ongoing debate within a tradition about the meaning of its shared beliefs, values, and customs that marks the distinction between a living tradition and one that has degenerated into dead usages.[33]

Until now our concern has been for the place of transcendental imagination in understanding other peoples and persons, and it remains to address the problem of self-understanding. In this regard internal understanding of others makes three indispensable contributions: it provides the differentiae that are a logical requirement of our individuation; it affords fuller understanding of our own qualities by showing us how they appear to others; and it apprises us by participatory enactment of unactualized possibilities in ourselves that others have actualized.

The logical requirement is expressed in Spinoza's dictum, "Omnis determinatio est negatio."[34] To be an individual is to be a distinctive one among others of one's kind, and knowledge of oneself as such entails knowledge of what one is not—the "is" and "is not" mutually implicate one another. Because the "is not" is extensively infinite, the knowledge of it that self-understanding requires cannot be perfect, but it achieves sufficiency by ordering the "is nots" according to types.

It is because we live not for ourselves alone but also for others

16

that others' viewpoints upon us are important to self-understanding. Here, again, because others represent a limitless extension, principles of economy must be employed, and the effective ones are "representative" others and "personally significant" others. Representative others enrich our self-understanding by disclosing valid aspects of the meanings of our thought and conduct that are other than their meaning for us. For personally significant others, consider someone we love. By relatively noncontroversial definition, our love for them means that (1) we desire their well-being for their sake; and (2) we want to ourselves contribute to their well-being. To contribute to their well-being, we must know not just what our conduct toward them means to us or what we intend it to mean to them, but what it in fact means to them—which is to say, their interpretation of it.

Finally, as I said above, from others we learn of our own unactualized possibilities, and the importance of this to self-knowledge is provided by Stuart Hampshire:

> A person . . . explains himself to himself by his history, but by his history as accompanied by unrealized possibilities. . . . His individual nature, and the quality of his life . . . emerge in the possibilities that were real possibilities for him, which he considered and rejected for some reason or other. From the moral point of view, it is even a significant fact about him . . . that a certain possibility, which might have occurred to him as a possibility, never actually did occur to him. In self-examination one may press this inquiry into possibilities very far, and this pressure upon possibility belongs to the essence of moral reflection.[35]

These three considerations support the conviction of Socrates that dialogue is an essential means for gaining self-knowledge; and they may lend support to Buber's stronger claim that participatory understanding of a Thou is a necessary precondition of the disclosure of the I.

Imagination and Stages of Personal Growth

I now want to introduce a developmental consideration in virtue of which transcendental imagination is indispensable to longitudinal

17

self-understanding, that is, to self-understanding over time by means of retrospection and anticipation. It is the consideration that maturation occurs by stages, within each of which growth is a continuum, while the transition between stages is a discontinuous exchange of perspectival worlds. The conception of development as a succession of stages, each with its distinctive developmental requirements, is as old as the Hindu Vedas and as current as the developmental psychologies of, for example, Piaget, Erikson, Maslow, William Perry, and Carol Gilligan.[36] In Emerson's words, "The soul's advances are not made by gradation, such as can be represented by motion in a straight line, but rather by ascension of state, such as can be represented by metamorphosis,—from the egg to the worm, from the worm to the fly."[37] The concept of human development by stages possesses, it seems to me, more explanatory power than the more prevalent continuum model, according to which persons' identities are the lifelong extrapolations of what they were in the beginning. For example, the autonomy that in some measure we associate—rightly, I think—with adult life cannot be the extrapolation of the dependence of infancy and childhood because autonomy and dependence are contradictory. In the stage concept, the emergence of autonomy displaces the prior dependence of childhood, and, in doing so, it transforms the light in which everything in the world appears to the individual.

According to the stage concept, each of us is a significantly different person at each stage of his or her life. The implication of this is that to recover the child one was, for example, is not a matter of working backward by inference along a growth continuum, but of exchanging one's adult perspective for one's perspective upon the world and oneself in one's childhood; it is an application of the historical method that Collingwood termed "imaginative reenactment."

Ordinary retrospection conceals discontinuous stage-exchanges by virtue of the capacity of the individual's present perspectival world to accommodate whatever is presented to it, including the individual's own past. A defect of the narrative theory of personal identity is that its requirement for narrative unity endorses an adult in the distortion of perceiving his or her own childhood and adolescence as prologue to the person he or she presently is.[38] In fact, each of these stages has its own story, recovery of which depends upon lending himself or herself to the viewpoint of the child and the adolescent he or she was, in exchange for his or her present perspective, and recovering his or her relations to the world in that identity.

In the forward direction, to grow from one stage to the next is to leave behind one's familiar world and enter *terra incognita* that calls for exploration. In Thoreau's words, "Not until we are lost, in other words, not till we have lost the world, do we begin to find ourselves, and realize where we are and the infinite extent of our relations."[39] To cross the threshold of adolescence, for example, is to leave behind the world of childhood for a new and bewildering world in which one must learn to make one's way, and it is to leave behind one's child-identity for a different identity of which one has as yet only fleeting intimations. Of course, it is not that one carries nothing of the prior stage into the next stage; it is that what one carries forward is significantly altered in meaning by stage-exchange.

Conceptions of individual development must take account of developmental arrest, developmental retardation, and developmental regression. Among contributing factors are the force of habit, the comforts of familiarity, and the pleasures of mastery that are experienced at the culmination of a well-lived stage but must be laboriously regained in the next stage. Resistance to the commitment that characterizes well-lived adulthood may reflect a reluctance to leave the delights of novelty that attend adolescent adventurousness. (Kierkegaard observed that commitment becomes attractive only when novelty itself loses its novelty.[40]) Correspondingly, the invitation to adventure at the threshold of adolescence encounters resistance in the desire to prolong the security of childhood in the womb of the family.

Innocent Parochialism to Dogmatic Absolutism

When resistance triumphs at the threshold of adolescence, the outcome is the perpetuation of childhood's parochialism. I will conclude this introduction by identifying the path from perpetuated parochialism to dogmatic absolutism. By "dogmatic absolutism" I refer not to the epistemological conviction that the idea of ultimate truth can be conceived or to the thesis that such a conception is a necessary "regulatory principle" without which the notion of "progress" would have no meaning, as Karl Popper suggests,[41] but to the claim by persons and parties to be in exclusive possession of absolute truth.

The explosive charge in dogmatic absolutism is its denigration of every alternative to itself. Throughout history the cost has been high, but it has become unbearable since Hiroshima and Nagasaki. To discredit dogmatic absolutism has become imperative in the interest of stabilizing interactive worlds of many and diverse cultures; and it is the part of philosophy to discredit the presuppositions that per- spectiveless (absolute) truth is accessible to human beings, and that for every valid question there is just one right answer. This will be undertaken in chapter 4. The first task is to account for the preva- lence of dogmatic absolutisms throughout human history, when they appear to fly in the face of the conspicuous facts of the fallibility and finitude of human beings. The conception of stages of development provides an explanation of dogmatic absolutism as the outgrowth of native parochialism that has lost its innocence and turned self- aggrandizing and aggressive.

The innocence of native parochialism is the innocence of child- hood. All children are parochial because, thanks to the essential de- pendence of childhood, they must be taught what to believe before they have developed the capacity for independent thought. It is the inevitability of parochialism in the beginning of every human life that led Santayana to call it "normal madness."[42] Initially a child mistakes the beliefs it is taught for the only beliefs possible, because it knows no other.

Intervening Factors: Emphasis on Adolescence

Three factors intervene in protracted sequence. First, the child dis- covers the existence of true alternatives to some of its beliefs and patterns of conduct; for example, he encounters a strangely garbed member of another tribe while hunting; she learns that some beliefs of the Jewish boy next door really do differ importantly from her own (let us say) Presbyterian beliefs. The second intervention is the initial stirrings within the child of autonomy, centering in the capacity for independent thought. The third is the onset of the adventurousness that announces adolescence, about which Robert Louis Stevenson would say, "Youth is wholly experimental."[43]

When these interventions are allowed to do their work, they transform the meaning of "otherness." Initially, the differences the child discovers are perceived by him or her as unrelated to the self, much in the way the child observes the variety of creatures at a zoo. The combined effect of autonomy and adventurousness is to convert disconnected "others" into possibilities for the self. Adolescence relentlessly poses the question, "What would it be like to be this other, and that other," because emerging autonomy from its beginning foreshadows the problem of eventually deciding upon one's adult course of life.

However, the developmental work of the three interventions can be suppressed, either by internal resistance to growth of such kinds as were noted above, or by adult authority. A primary objective of an authoritarian family or an authoritarian society is to condition its children for the purpose of laying down their adult courses of life. Conditioning eliminates options in two ways: it produces young people who are equipped only for the course of life they are expected to pursue; and it inculcates the belief that the alternatives are misguided, perverse, or evil. This is the posture of dogmatic absolutism.

Political historians have sometimes expressed puzzlement over the priority with which totalitarian regimes take control of the arts, when, after all, the arts "bake no bread." The totalitarian aim is, in this respect, unerring, for the arts are the work of an imagination that envisages inviting alternatives to whatever happens presently to exist. In the paradigmatic case of Plato's *Republic*, an enduring enigma to scholars has been: Why is Plato, himself a poet, so seemingly hostile to poets and poetry in his blueprint of the ideal state? The answer is because Plato fully appreciates the power and the purpose of presenting alternatives to whatever presently exists, and regards this as subversive of the single-minded convictions that he thinks the republic requires. In short, what the republic presents is the view of poetry of Plato as political theorist. John Herman Randall

21

is therefore profoundly correct when he says that Plato's theory of poetry as such "is not to be found in the *Republic*, Book X, in the discussion of *mimesis*, imitation. This discussion is *not* about poetry, but about what happens to poetry in the efficiently organized state, where it becomes mere 'imitation'—in modern terms, where it is limited to 'socialist realism'—or its stereotyped perversions."[44]

Plato was indeed of two minds about poetry, but he was not in the least confused, ambivalent, or undecided, as much critical opinion has it. In the *Republic* and the *Laws*, he presents poetry from the standpoint of politics; elsewhere he presents poetry for what it is in itself. Poetry is a danger in particular to authoritarian politics because it presents not falsehoods but alternative truths.

If the foregoing analysis of individual development is correct, there can be no release from the innocent parochialism in which every life begins without the employment of transcendental imagination. Innocent parochialism, if it is not disrupted by the recognition of valid alternatives, readily becomes the dogmatic absolutism that humankind can no longer afford. Given its dedication to this outcome, authoritarianism unerringly works to extinguish transcendental imagination; but because transcendental imagination is initially within all persons as a latent capacity that must be developed, its systemic neglect in a society's pattern of education has a high likelihood of producing the same result.

Looming squarely in our path at this point is the currently prevalent thesis that human beings are necessarily and irremediably ethnocentric. In one of its forms it precludes the exchanges of perspectival worlds that we have identified as the function of transcendental imagination. Since it would make of our inquiry a nonstarter, this form of the thesis will be examined in the next chapter.

Notes

1. Eva T. H. Brann, *The World of the Imagination: Sum and Substance* (Savage, Md.: Rowman & Littlefield, 1991).
2. William James, *The Will to Believe and Other Essays in Popular Philos-*

ophy, ed. Frederick H. Burkhart, Fredson Bowers, and Ignas K. Skrupskelis (Cambridge: Harvard University Press, 1979), Appendix IV, p. 438.

3. John Kekes, *The Morality of Pluralism* (Princeton: Princeton University Press, 1993), p. 101. Chapter 6, "Possibilities of Life," is a scrupulous and insightful study of moral imagination that I will draw upon for several important points.

4. Abraham H. Maslow, *Toward a Psychology of Being*, 2d ed. (New York: D. Van Nostrand, 1968), p. 15.

5. A. O. Lovejoy, *The Great Chain of Being* (Cambridge: Harvard University Press, 1936), e.g., chap. 4, "The Principle of Plenitude and the New Cosmography."

6. Clarence Irving Lewis, *Mind and the World Order: Outline of a Theory of Knowledge* (New York: Dover Publications, 1956), pp. 197, 227, 225.

7. *Heauton Timoroumenos*, act 1, scene 1, line 25.

8. Henri Bergson, *Laughter*, in *Comedy*, ed. Wylie Sypher (Garden City, N.Y.: Doubleday Anchor Books, 1956), p. 162.

9. George Santayana, *Realism of Being*, one vol. ed. (New York: Charles Scribner's Sons, 1942), p. xiii.

10. Maurice Mandelbaum contends that a perspectivist who claims that he "can escape the limitations of his own perspective" is committing the "fallacy of self-exemption"—see Mandelbaum, "Subjective, Objective, and Conceptual Relativisms," *Relativism, Cognitive and Moral*, in eds. Jack W. Meiland and Michael Krausz (Notre Dame: University of Notre Dame Press, 1982), p. 43. But this would be true only if the perspectivist were claiming that in transcending the limitations of his own perspective he arrived at perspectiveless knowledge. To claim, as I do, that by transcending the limitations of one's own perspective one lands in an alternative perspective is not to claim exemption from perspectival knowledge.

Using Benjamin Whorf's contention that different perspectival worlds are shaped by the Indo-European languages and the Navajo language, Mandelbaum says, "Yet, even though Whorf was brought up on Indo-European languages, with the logic of his thinking presumably dependent on the grammatical structure of these languages, he was able to understand how nature appeared to the Apache. In short, as a linguist, he was not bound by his own grammar, but stood outside both his own language and theirs" (Meiland and Krausz, p. 49). But, in the first place, for Whorf to understand how nature appears to the Navajos, it is necessary for Whorf to stand inside their language, not outside it. Moreover, he can then describe how it appears to Navajos to readers of English, for example, because in that language it is a possible meaning that is not the accepted meaning. For a native English speaker to accept

23

the Navajo meaning would entail pervasive revisions in the English speaker's perspective, amounting to a transformation. An analogous case within a single language system would be a feminist perspective as presented to a male chauvinist; he can understand it sufficiently to recognize that to *accept* it will require transforming other beliefs that he holds, which in turn will affect still other beliefs, and so on.

So Whorf does not commit the self-exempting fallacy by claiming to have entered the Navajo world of meanings or by making that world at least partially intelligible (as an inoperative alternative) to English speakers. Moreover he would not be committing the self-exempting fallacy by claiming to stand outside both the Navajo perspective and the English-speaking perspective so long as he acknowledged that his adopted standpoint *was* a standpoint, that is, another perspective.

11. Plato, *Timaeus*, 71.

12. Clifford Geertz, *The Interpretation of Cultures* (New York: Basic Books, 1973), p. 14.

13. Ibid., p. 15.

14. Ibid., pp. 15–16.

15. Ibid., p. 5.

16. R. G. Collingwood, *The Idea of History* (New York: Oxford University Press Galaxy Books, 1956), p. 215.

17. Collingwood differs importantly from Geertz, Scheler, and Buber by holding that only ideas, and not other subjective content (perceptions, feelings, volitions), can be imaginatively reenacted. This is because other subjective content is, according to Collingwood, wholly immediate and thus fugitive, whereas ideas, together with their partial element of irrecoverable immediacy, are also universal and timeless.

This thesis has the paradoxical effect of making the subject matter of history ahistorical, and I think it also contradicts Collingwood's insistence that it is the ideas of the particular personages under study that history must recover. If the Archimedean Principle, for example, is identical in every mind that thinks it, then it is devoid of the particular personage of Archimedes. To press the point: had Euclid discovered one of the non-Euclidean geometries, the discovery would have significantly altered the status in which he held his "Euclidean" axioms.

Moreover, I think the recoverability of feelings (for example) is evident to each of us in our own cases. My recollection of a shameful incident in my past can reproduce in me the shame I felt then, and similarly for past incidents of joy, contentment, anger, and the rest. If thought, feeling, perception, and volition are interdependent, as I believe they are, then it is a fallacy of abstraction to attempt to treat one of them in disregard of the others.

18. Collingwood, *The Idea of History*, pp. 242–43.

19. Ibid., pp. 244–45.

20. Ibid., p. 246.

21. R. M. Hare, *Moral Thinking, Its Levels, Methods, and Point* (Oxford: Oxford University Press, 1981), p. 92.

22. Ibid., p. 94.

23. Ibid., pp. 119, 121.

24. Martin Buber, *I and Thou*, trans. Walter Kaufmann (New York: Charles Scribner's Sons, 1970), p. 59.

25. Martin Buber, *The Knowledge of Man*, trans. Maurice Friedman and Ronald Gregor Smith (New York: Harper Torchbooks, 1965), p. 70.

26. Max Scheler, *The Nature of Sympathy*, trans. Peter Heath (London: Routledge & Kegan Paul, 1954), pp. 167–68.

27. Ibid., p. 49.

28. Samuel Taylor Coleridge, notebook entry 2441, cited in Mary Warnock, *Imagination* (Berkeley: University of California Press, 1976), p. 81.

29. Hare, *Moral Thinking*, p. 65.

30. Samuel Taylor Coleridge, *Biographia Literaria* (London: J. M. Dent & Sons, Everyman's Library, 1965), p. 169.

31. Bertrand Russell, *A History of Western Philosophy* (New York: Simon & Schuster, 1945), p. 39.

32. Geertz, *The Interpretation of Cultures*, pp. 40–41.

33. For example, Emile Durkheim, *Moral Education*, trans. Everett K. Wilson and Herman Schnurer (New York: The Free Press, 1973), Part I; Michael Oakeshott, "On Being Conservative," in *Rationalism in Politics and Other Essays* (Totowa, N. J.: Rowman & Littlefield, 1977), pp. 168–96 and Alasdair MacIntyre, *After Virtue* (Notre Dame: University of Notre Dame Press, 1981), chap. 15.

34. Benedict de Spinoza, *Opera* (Heidelberg, 1925), IV, p. 240 (Epistolae L). See also, First Scholium to the Eighth Proposition, Part I, *Ethics*.

35. Stuart Hampshire, *Innocence and Experience* (Cambridge: Harvard University Press, 1989), p. 101.

36. See, e.g., Jean Piaget, *The Moral Judgment of the Child*, trans. Marjorie Gabain (Glencoe, Ill.: The Free Press, 1932), chap. 4; Erik H. Erikson, *Childhood and Society*, 2d ed. (New York: W. W. Norton, 1963), chap. 8; Abraham H. Maslow, *Toward a Psychology of Being*, Part II; William G. Perry, *Forms of Intellectual and Ethical Growth in the College Years* (New York: Holt, Rinehart, and Winston, 1968); Lawrence Kohlberg, *The Philosophy of Moral Development* (New York: Harper & Row, 1981); Carol Gilligan, *In a Different Voice* (Cambridge: Harvard University Press, 1982), chap. 3.

37. Ralph Waldo Emerson, "The Over-Soul," *Complete Works* (Boston & New York: Houghton Mifflin, 1903), vol. 2, p. 274.

38. Among prominent recent proponents of the narrative theory of identity are Alasdair MacIntyre, *After Virtue*, chap. 15; Robert N. Bellah et al., *Habits of the Heart* (Berkeley: University of California Press, 1985), e.g., p. 81; David Carr, *Time, Narrative, and History* (Bloomington: Indiana University Press, 1986); Edwin Muir, *An Autobiography* (New York: William Sloane Associates, 1954), chap. 1.; Nicholas Berdaiev, *Dream and Reality* (London: Blies, 1950). Muir and Berdaiev are commendably sensitive to the various forms of self-deception to which a narrative identity is susceptible.

39. Henry D. Thoreau, *Walden*, ed. J. Lyndon Shanley (Princeton: Princeton University Press, 1971), p. 171.

40. I am referring to Kierkegaard's thesis that "aesthetic despair," which terminates the delights of novelty in the aesthetic or "Don Juan" stage, is boredom. See Soren Kierkegaard, *Either/Or*, trans. David F. and Lillian Marvin Swenson (New York: Doubleday Anchor Books, 1959), vol. 1; see the chapter entitled "The Immediate Stages of the Erotic, or the Musical Erotic."

41. Karl Popper, e.g., "Truth and Approximation to Truth," in *Popper Selections*, ed. David Miller (Princeton: Princeton University Press, 1985), p. 185.

42. George Santayana, "Normal Madness," in *Dialogues in Limbo* (New York: Charles Scribner's Sons, 1925).

43. Robert Louis Stevenson, "Letter to a Young Gentleman," in *Across the Plains* (New York: Charles Scribner's Sons, 1904), p. 272.

44. John Herman Randall, *Plato: Dramatist of the Life of Reason* (New York: Columbia University Press, 1970), p. 145n.

Chapter 2

IS ETHNOCENTRISM INESCAPABLE?

To say that human beings are irremediably ethnocentric may have either of two meanings. One of them, if correct, precludes the function that was attributed to transcendental imagination in chapter 1. Before undertaking further study of that function, we must see if ethnocentrism is genuinely a roadblock in our path.

Human beings might be irremediably ethnocentric in the sense that they are inevitably situated in a cultural "web of significance"; or they might be so in the sense that they are inescapably situated in the particular cultural web of significance in which their patterns of thought and conduct were initially shaped. The former meaning accommodates the exchanges of perspectival worlds that were identified as the function of transcendental imagination in chapter 1, while denying, as we have done, that persons have access to perspectiveless knowledge. If every person's original received perspective is inescapable, then perspectival exchange is not possible. It is this proposal that requires our attention.

Two Meanings of Ethnocentrism

What I will term "inescapable-received-ethnocentrism" also has two importantly different forms. One form, as advanced by Donald Davidson, is the claim that the notion of incommensurably alternative perspectival worlds is incoherent.[1] If this is so, then there cannot be multiplicity of the kind that calls transcendental imagination into play. Davidson's case rests upon a definition of "incommensurable" that I will challenge shortly.

In contrast to Davidson, Richard Rorty and Michael Krausz affirm the existence of alternative perspectival worlds but hold that each person is irremediably bound to view them through his or her received perspective. (From this common ground, Krausz and Rorty draw importantly different implications that will be considered in chapter 4.)

In both forms, inescapable-received-ethnocentrism contends that it cannot be other than "our lights" by which we perceive, conceptualize, and judge other persons and cultures; and this precludes the "internal" knowledge of others that was called "understanding" in chapter 1. According to Davidson, there are

> limits to how much individual or social systems of thought can differ.
> . . . Of course there are contrasts from epoch to epoch, from culture to
> culture, and person to person of kinds which we all recognize and strug-
> gle with; but these are contrasts which, with sympathy and effort, we
> can explain and understand. Trouble comes when we try to embrace the
> idea that there might be more comprehensive differences, for this seems
> (absurdly) to ask us to take up a stance outside our own ways of
> thought.[2]

The thesis that it is only in our own terms that we can understand others is shared by Hilary Putnam, Rorty, and Krausz. According to Putnam, "the whole justification of an interpretive scheme . . . is that it renders the behavior of others at least minimally reasonable by our lights."[3] Commending this, Rorty says that, thus, "the notion of 'local cultural norms' will lose its offensively parochial overtones. For now to say that we must work by our own lights, that we must be ethnocentric, is merely to say that beliefs suggested by another culture must be tested by trying to weave them together with beliefs we already have."[4] Similarly, Krausz says, "In sum, while critical comparison between interpretations of cultures is possible, it is ineliminably tied to one's own culture. Whatever good reasons that can be generated for one's preference for a given interpretation must arise within one's own culture. Who else's would they be?"[5]

According to Davidson (but not to Rorty or Krausz) our own lights are not just the only lights available to us, they are the only lights humanly possible.

> What matters is this: if all we know is what sentences a speaker holds true, and we cannot assume that his language is our own, then we cannot take even a first step towards interpretation without knowing or assuming a great deal about the speaker's beliefs. Since knowledge of beliefs comes only with the ability to interpret words, the only possibility at the start is to assume general agreement on beliefs.[6]

Davidson identifies this assumption with the "charity" that Willard Van Orman Quine proposes as a necessary condition of translation.[7] In Davidson's words, "Charity is forced on us;—whether we like it or not, if we want to understand others, we must count them right on most matters."[8] In Davidson's reading, the matters in which we are to count them right are ones on which all persons must be presumed to agree. The effect of this is that at the basic level, "charity" toward others does not entail lending ourselves to their viewpoint but presupposing their agreement with us.

Davidson's claimed necessity of presuming general agreement on beliefs draws the following response from Alasdair MacIntyre:

> The danger of contemporary antirelativism . . . is that it suggests that what is in fact a contingent social condition whose limitations it is important for us to overcome is in fact a necessary condition of rational social existence. For antirelativism pictures us first as necessarily inhabiting our own conceptual scheme, our own *Weltanschauung*. ("Whose conceptual scheme, whose *Weltanschauung* but our own could we be expected to inhabit?" is the rhetorical question that is sometimes posed), and second as necessarily acquiring whatever understanding we may possess of the

conceptual schemes and *Weltanschauungen* of others by a process of translation so conceived that any intelligible rendering of the concepts and beliefs of the others must represent them as in all central respects similar to our own.[9]

This danger stands out in bold relief in Davidson's suggestion that if concepts and beliefs were to be significantly unlike ours, they would not be concepts and beliefs. In his words, "We know what states of mind are like, and how they are correctly identified; they are just those states whose contents can be discovered in well-known ways. If other people or creatures are in states not discoverable by these methods, it can be, not because our methods fail us, but because those states are not correctly called states of mind—they are not beliefs, desires, wishes, or intentions."[10]

However, states of mind that can be discovered in well-known ways are well-known states of mind. Unfamiliar states of mind require exceptional methods. In my thesis of chapter 1, we can discover unfamiliar states of mind by participatory enactment of the worlds in which they are familiar states of mind. We can do this because our familiar world together with our personal identity within it are interpretations that have alternatives. We can exchange our familiar interpretive world for alternative interpretive worlds by imaginatively actualizing alternative possibilities, a process that entails in ourselves imaginative identity-exchange. Such imaginative identity-exchange occurs, for example, when we identify with the protagonist of a novel or a play who is very different from ourselves, and if human beings lacked this capacity, fictional literature could not have the liberalizing effect that constitutes much of its educational value.

Incommensurability, Untranslatability, and Incompossibility

Davidson assumes that a conceptual scheme that is incommensurable with our own is "forever beyond our grasp," and says that such an idea is "meaningless . . . due simply to what we mean by a system of concepts."[11] The assumption comes from Davidson's

30

equation of "incommensurable" with "totally untranslatable," which is to say "wholly unintelligible." If this were so, then to hold that there are incommensurable conceptual schemes would be to claim knowledge of what is by definition unknowable.

My countercontention is that we can know of the existence of conceptual schemes alternative to our own (I use the term "perspectives" to indicate that not just concepts but also percepts, feelings, and volitions are involved) because we have sufficient access to them to recognize that we cannot *accept* them while retaining our own. For example, consider a characteristic feminist declaration—say, "Equal pay for equal work"—as presented to a male chauvinist. He rejects it, not because it is unintelligible to him, but because he understands it sufficiently to recognize that to accept it would entail sweeping changes throughout his system of beliefs, and also his patterns of conduct (for example, voting in favor instead of against the Equal Rights Amendment) and of feeling (centering in his sympathies and antipathies, starting with his antipathy to the declaration "Equal pay for equal work"). Similarly, a pantheistic understanding of religion is not wholly unintelligible to a religious dualist but cannot be accepted by him or her without sending transformative reverberations throughout his or her integrated system of beliefs, conduct, and feelings.

The situation is analogous where different language systems are involved. In MacIntyre's words, "It is not that the beliefs of each community cannot be represented in any way at all in the language of the other; it is rather that the outcome in each case of rendering those beliefs sufficiently intelligible to be evaluated by a member of the other community involves characterizing those beliefs in such a way that they are bound to be rejected."[12]

Partial intelligibility of belief systems alternative to one's own has two possible explanations, one of them piecemeal and the other holistic. In the piecemeal account, some expressions in system A are fully intelligible in the terms of system B but other expressions are not. In the holistic account, any expression in one system is partially intelligible in the other, but because the parts of a system gain meaning by mutual implication with other parts, full understanding of any part requires understanding of the whole.

It is not necessary here to decide between the two accounts, piece-meal and holistic, because the basic point is the same: incommensurability exists between belief systems that cannot be simultaneously *accepted*. It accommodates the partial intelligibility that affords the evidence that they cannot be simultaneously accepted; and the presence of this partial intelligibility overturns Davidson's definition of incommensurability as complete untranslatability and therefore total unintelligibility. (His argument for the incoherence of the idea of alternative conceptual schemes only works if "beyond our grasp" means entirely so.) My conclusion is that it is a mistake to follow the "linguistic turn" in defining "incommensurability" as "untranslatability," and I propose instead "incompossibility" in the meaning of "cannot coexist in the same subject at the same time."

In this light, Davidson is mistaken to suppose that Benjamin Whorf inadvertently demonstrated the commensurability of the Hopi worldview and the worldview of English speakers by translating some Hopi sentences into English, and he is correspondingly mistaken to suppose that Thomas Kuhn refuted his own thesis regarding scientific revolutions by "saying what things were like before the revolution using—what else?—our post-revolutionary idiom."[13] To be sure, complete understanding of the Hopi worldview or of Aristotelian physics (or of any element of either, if holism is correct) is nothing short of understanding the whole. The accomplishment of Whorf and Kuhn is to use partial translatability to disclose incompossibility.

If incommensurability means incompossibility, what bars our access to alternative perspectival worlds is our allegiance to our own, and contrary to the thesis of inescapable-received-ethnocentrism, this is not of necessity "forever." It obtains so long as that allegiance is maintained. Quite certainly that allegiance can be maintained come what may by what C. S. Peirce named "the method of tenacity."[14] Then alternative beliefs and patterns of conduct will be viewed intractably by "our lights," and we are in the condition of the traveler described by Emerson: "I pack my trunk, embrace my friends, embark on the sea and at last wake up in Naples, and there beside me is the stern fact, the sad self, unrelenting, identical, that I fled from."[15] But by the imaginative actualization of other possibilities within ourselves, we have the option of entering alternative perspectival worlds by setting aside our "home" perspective and our accustomed self-understanding. What incompossibility means is that we cannot occupy two incommensurable perspectival worlds at the same time.

In turning to the Krausz-Rorty version of the thesis of inescapable-received-ethnocentrism, I will begin by giving closer attention to the meaning of "our lights" and also to the meanings of "possibility," "impossibility," and "incompossibility" that I am employing, for example when I spoke just above of an "option" and a "cannot."

"Our Lights"

In one sense, everything we experience is "ours," but that we recognize a deeper sense will be evident from the following example. Suppose that you are suddenly thrust into a radically novel situation and for a time experience the bewilderment that typically befalls us on such occasions. At such a time we commonly say that we must "sort out" our thoughts and feelings, and the saying is apt because bewilderment is not absence of thoughts and feelings but a disordered deluge of them, some of which are likely to be novel in response to the novelty of the situation.

In this condition all of the thoughts and feelings that we experience are "ours" in the obvious sense that it is we who experience them, but what we seek in our sorting out is the thoughts and feelings that we will make ours in the deeper sense that we identify with them and act upon them. This is my first point. The experience of bewilderment is the experience of a deluge of thoughts and feelings that are not ours in the deeper sense of self-identification, and it attests to our access to thoughts and feelings that are not ours in that sense. They are accessible to us because they subsist as possibilities within ourselves. As such they can be actualized, not just in bewilderment, but deliberately by our imaginative identification with persons whose thoughts and feelings they are, in the second sense of self-identification.

It was to introduce people to unactualized possibilities in them-

33

selves that Kurt Hahn employed deliberate bewilderment as a peda-
gogical device in the Outward Bound schools of which he was the
founder. The effect of thrusting enrollees into novel and challenging
environments is, Hahn knew, to force them to relinquish their habitual thoughts, feelings, and strategies and seek out replacements for
their new circumstances. Nothing in the tool kits they bring from
home works. It was because Hahn recognized the strength in the
grip of the familiar that he adopted his motto: "Students must be
impelled into experiences."[16] Hahn seized the opportunity presented
by the native adventurousness of adolescence to disrupt the process
by which habit converts the innocent parochialism of childhood into
the entrenched parochialism of which George Santayana says, "The
philosophy of the common man is an old wife that gives him no
pleasure, yet he cannot live without her, and resents any aspersions
that strangers may cast on her character."[17]

The second point is that when we identify ourselves with certain
thoughts, feelings, desires, aspirations, and aversions, the identification may be either experimental and exploratory or committed and
formative. For example, when a reader of a novel identifies with its
protagonist—say, Lewis Eliot in C. P. Snow's *The Masters*—it is in
order to experience the setting and events of the narrative as a par-
ticipant, but with full knowledge that he will resume his customary
identity upon putting the book aside. In the same way, historians'
identifications with participants in events of the past and anthropol-
ogists' identifications with subjects in other cultures are experimental
and exploratory, in contrast to their committed self-identifications in
their home cultures.

For convenience I will term a person's exploratory identifications
"hypothetical," and his or her home identification "categorical."
Hypothetical identification deactivates the categorical "us" and its
perspectival world in favor of a hypothetical "us" that had until the
experiment been a "them." "Their lights" are now "our lights" for
the duration of the hypothetical identification, but that "their lights"
can become "our lights" is denied by proponents of the Krausz-
Rorty version of inescapable-received-ethnocentrism. The rhetorical
question put by proponents of inescapable-received-ethnocentrism,
"Whose lights but ours could they be?," appears decisive only when

the difference between hypothetical and categorical self-identification is disregarded.

My thesis is that our categorical identity represents the actualization within us of certain possibilities that are surrounded by unactualized possibilities. As biologically underdetermined beings who are neotenus—born in an embryonic condition and destined to a lengthy dependence—our initial formation occurs through the processes of enculturation in childhood, and personal choice plays no significant part in it. However, subsequent to childhood our discovery of other possibilities in ourselves is our recognition that we might be other than our enculturation has formed us, and emergent autonomy introduces personal choice into the ongoing processes of identity formation. One purpose in our study of persons different from ourselves is to understand them; but a second purpose is the disclosure such study affords of unrecognized possibilities in ourselves, which is an essential part of self-understanding as Stuart Hampshire contended in *Innocence and Experience* (see chap. 1).

The study of other persons contributes to self-understanding only when the possibilities that they have actualized are perceived as possibilities for oneself. Where their actualized possibilities are commensurable with one's own, the relationship is merely additive, but where their possibilities are incommensurable with our own, they can be entertained as our own only by substitution. The term I am employing for the disparity in such cases between "their lights" and "our lights" is "compossibility." Their lights become our lights by the experimental exchange of our perspectival world and our identity within it for theirs, through the exercise of transcendental imagination.

Impossibility

My defense of transcendental imagination as a capacity of human beings obliges me to distinguish incompossibility from logical impossibility and psychological impossibility. Logical impossibility attends the bipolar condition of contradiction: it is logically impossible for something to be both A and not-A in the same respect at the same

35

time. However, the condition of the impossibility of occupying two perspectival worlds at the same time is not bipolar but multivalent: world A confronts not-A worlds B, C, D, E, et al. As was argued in chapter 1, incompossibility obtains because each world is a distinctive perspective upon the whole of actual and possible experience. This is to say that a perspectival world is a plenum without lacunae, from which it follows that ignorance is not a void but a presence, though the presence may be either explicit or implicit. Whatever has not yet appeared in a perspectival world has a place (a meaning) awaiting it if and when it should appear—this is what is meant by "implicit presence." To be sure, world B is made up of meanings that are not present in world A, but world A has implicit meanings in readiness for those meanings. For a meaning from world B to appear as its B-meaning in world A would require displacement of a meaning that is present either explicitly or implicitly in world A. What makes A a "world" is the interconnectedness of the meanings that compose it. Accordingly, such displacement cannot be piecemeal but entails the displacement of everything else in the A-world by everything from the B-world—the phenomenon of perspectival world-exchange. As chapter 1 was designed to show, the possibility of perspectival world-exchange is attested to by examples of its occurrence together with the theory that renders such examples intelligible. Here our purpose has been to show that incompossibility precludes simultaneous occupation of alternative perspectival worlds but does not preclude occupation of two or more such worlds successively.

In the same way, the impossibility of living different courses of life at the same time is not that of logical contradiction, as for example the logical impossibility in being a married bachelor. It is the incompossibility that obtains because different courses of life each carry entailments that lead in different directions. Different courses of life can be lived by a given individual successively but not simultaneously.

Examples of perspectival world-exchange (e.g., Augustine's conversion from paganism to Christianity; the conversions of early twentieth-century physicists from a Newtonian to an Einsteinian world; the conversion of young people from the world of childhood to the world of adolescence) demonstrate the possibility of such ex-change for human beings in principle, but leave open the question of whether or not circumstances may foreclose the possibility in par-ticular cases. It is the question of contingent psychological obstruc-tions that I want to address, but I will begin with the most obvious contingency, that of acquaintance.

A person who has never heard of the Hopi is prevented by lack of acquaintance from imaginatively adopting their perspectival world. Throughout human history, there have been countless persons whose acquaintance has been restricted to their own culture and even to their insular regional subculture. But within every culture and sub-culture, no matter how insular, are to be found disparate perspecti-val worlds, for example in many cases the disparate male and female worlds, or those of the country and the town, or of the rich and the poor. Moreover, as William James argued, disparate perspectival worlds are constructed by disparate temperaments. For his example he distinguished the interpretive worlds of what he termed the "tender-minded" and the "tough-minded" temperaments, and the case is no less applicable to such disparities as the choleric and the sanguine, the extroverted and the introverted, and so on.[18] In short, the possibility of perspectival exchanges is seldom if ever precluded by lack of proximate alternatives. It may be precluded by psychosis or severe mental retardation in either the object or the agent of the exchange, but these will be exceptions to any general understanding of humankind.

We speak of some persons as "imaginative" and others as "un-imaginative," but before invoking psychological incapacity to ac-count for the latter it will be well to notice the human propensity to employ "I can't" in instances where it is "I won't" that is descriptive. An explanation of this is provided by Jean-Paul Sartre: "I can't" attempts to evade self-responsibility by denying the freedom that self-responsibility presupposes.[19] For likely instances of it in the mat-ter of perspectival exchange, consider the man or woman who says that he or she "just can't understand" the opposite sex; or the het-erosexual who says that he or she can't begin to understand a gay person. That no impassable gulf exists in the first case is attested by novelists who successfully present the perspectival worlds of protagonists of their novels whose sex is the opposite of the author's. In the second case, it would be negligent on the part of inquiry to overlook the discomfort or disgust that is a prevalent response to homoeroticism by heterosexuals. In general, the human propensity to substitute "I can't" for "I refuse to," "I choose not to," "I deem it not worthwhile to," and so on, is such that inquiry that begins by seeking factors that will account for the various forms of "I won't" will often be successful. What remains of psychological impossibility will not overturn the thesis that perspectival exchange is a human capacity whose exercise is important to worthy living.

A type of necessity that in some sense precludes alternative courses of conduct is exemplified by Martin Luther's "Here I stand; I can do no other," and by Socrates' determination to continue to practice philosophy in Athens though it should cost him his life. It is termed "moral" (as distinguished from metaphysical, causal, and logical) necessity because it is a product of the will of the individual and not the nullification of it. Accordingly, moral necessity is literally a case of "won't" rather than "can't," and as distinguished from the evasions of self-responsibility that were considered just above, moral necessity is the expression of self-responsibility. Moral necessity must also be distinguished from Peirce's "method of tenacity," which is a means for thoughtlessly rejecting every opportunity for gaining internal knowledge of others. The tenacity in moral necessity is in respect to a chosen course of life that recognizes itself to be such. It in no way precludes imaginative identification with alternative courses of life but, on the contrary, presupposes internal knowledge of alternatives as a condition of true choice. Its commitment is not thoughtless but is supported by good reasons—for example, that in one's chosen course of life one has work to do that is valuable to others and satisfying to oneself. What internal knowledge of alternatives affords is recognition that others' commitments to courses of life different from one's own may likewise be supported by good reasons. This is an epistemic condition that is termed "multiplism" by Michael Krausz and will be considered in detail in chapter 4. It obtains when to a given question there are multiple "admissible" (Krausz's term to avoid the implied exclusivity of "right") answers, each of which is supportable by reasons that are good but not conclusive, which is to say they do not preclude admissible alternative answers.[20]

On the matter of perspectival world-exchange, Krausz identifies a contingent hazard that he thinks may eliminate it as a "live option" for many or most persons even if it is possible in principle. "Successfully conducting such an experiment . . . might require [a person] to project himself in a cultural context so different from his own that it would be an open question whether he could, in that scenario, continue to recognize himself as the culturally embodied person that he is."[21] I think it is not troublesome that such a person cannot *at the same time* recognize himself both in his adopted identity and his home identity, since the purpose of the experiment is to explore the perspectival world of his adopted identity. Nor, I think, is there a daunting risk that he will be unable to recover his home identity when he wishes, because this amounts to the recovery of deeply ingrained patterns of thought, feeling, and conduct. As we have argued, the incommensurability of perspectival worlds does not preclude successive occupation of two or more. Moreover, alternation between perspectival worlds can be quite rapid, as may be necessary in order that an anthropologist or an historian, for example, remain anthropologist or historian while engaged in the internal exploration of a perspectival world under study. An example of such alternation is the common practice of writers to "step back" from their work at intervals to view it in the adopted identities of the various classes of readers for whom it is intended. The practice operationalizes the obligation to "know your audience."

To summarize on "can't" versus "won't": the in-principle possibility of perspectival world exchange for human beings is demonstrated by actual occasions of it in human lives, for example, religious revelation and conversion, or the transformation of the world of one's childhood into the very different world of one's adolescence. The intelligibility of such exchanges is provided by the theoretical consideration that perspectival worlds, like the identities of persons that they both form and reflect, are the actualization of certain possibilities when other possibilities might have been actualized instead. To imaginatively explore an alternative world is to experimentally adopt an alternative identity. While contingent obstacles to such exchanges are real enough, they for the most part represent not true impossibilities, but difficulties of greater and lesser degree. To be sure, difficulties of extreme severity can render an individual's prospect of exploring alternative worlds so highly improbable as to represent what for practical purposes may be regarded as impossibility; but most of the difficulties are such that they can be overcome. My purpose in this book is to show that the capacity in persons of transcendental imagination promises gains that warrant a concerted attack upon the obstacles. Where investigation discloses the existence of contingent difficulties of such severity as to effectively prevent the employment of transcendental imagination—extreme poverty and rigidly authoritarian upbringing and education are candidates— concerted social effort should be directed to removing, diminishing, or counteracting such obstructions.

Other Minds

For Davidson, just as there can be no genuine disparity between cultural perspectives, so in the same way there can be none between minds, and the vexed philosophical "problem of other minds" rests upon a mistake. In his words, "Perhaps it is obvious that if the account I have sketched of our understanding of language, and its connection with the contents of thought, is correct, the accessibility of the minds of others is assured from the start."[22] At this point, he relies not on his deductive argument that the idea of a mind "forever beyond our reach" is incoherent, but on the "natural history" of what is in persons' heads. The natural history he cites is the enculturation by which children acquire words, propositions, beliefs, and patterns of conduct. He says,

> It is a commonplace of the empirical tradition that we learn our first words (which at the start serve the function of sentences)—words like "apple", "man", "dog", "water"— through a conditioning of sounds or verbal behavior to appropriate bits of matter in the public domain. . . . This is not just a story about how we learn to use words: it must also be

an essential part of an adequate account of what words refer to and what they mean.

He adds, "Needless to say, the whole story cannot be this simple. On the other hand, it is hard to believe that this sort of direct interaction between language users and public events and objects is not a basic part of the whole story, the part that, directly or indirectly, largely determines how words are related to things. Yet the story entails consequences that seem to have been ignored until very recently."[23]

The ignored consequence that receives Davidson's attention is "the demise of the subjective as previously conceived."[24] What he refers to as the previous conception is that of a subjectivity that excludes objectivity, leaving it a private space without apparent public access. Against this the "natural history" of subjectivity discloses it to be the internalization of public contents, from which Davidson concludes that persons can access one another's subjective content through the public contents that have been internalized. In his words, "others [can] learn what we think by noting the causal dependencies [those disclosed by the indicated 'natural history'] that give our thoughts their content."[25]

Obviously, this leaves out of account differences in patterns of enculturation among differing cultures, but by Davidson's argument that we must assume "general agreement on beliefs," there can be no incommensurable differences; and we are left with only such differences as "with sympathy and effort, we can explain and understand" in our own terms. To this I have presented my counterargument: Davidson's case is directed against incommensurability in the meaning of "totally untranslatable and therefore totally unintelligible," and does not touch its meaning as incompossible.

Davidson's supposition that "others can learn what we think" at any time in our lives by noting the public contents that we internalized as children overlooks the opportunity of significant alteration of this initial enculturated subjective content that arises with emergent autonomy beginning in adolescence. Autonomy, as I will use the term here, is the capacity for independent thinking and self-directed living. By its exercise, subjective content ceases to mirror public beliefs, feelings, desires, wishes, and intentions, and is transformed by self-awareness, self-examination, self-criticism, and exploratory discovery of alternatives. The possible transformations are of two basic kinds: evolutionary and revolutionary. By evolutionary transformation the initial subjective content is developed; but because it can be developed in innumerable ways, it is not possible to arrive at its development by a particular individual merely from the public content that that individual internalized in his or her dependent childhood.

For examples of evolutionary transformation, consider the mature theology of Soren Kierkegaard or Paul Tillich. Kierkegaard arrived at the explosive conclusion that faith is "the teleological suspension of the ethical," and Tillich arrived at the heterodox conception of God as "a symbol of a symbol."[26] Both theologies were developed out of an initial enculturation in orthodox Protestant Christianity, but it is impossible to access the mature thought of either Kierkegaard or Tillich out of this initial "causal dependency" because of their subsequent innovative thinking.

By revolutionary transformation I refer to the abandonment of one or more aspects of one's initially enculturated subjective content and its displacement by incompossible alternatives. To be sure, it remains unalterably the case that one's initially enculturated subjective content was just what it was; it is one's relationship to it that is changed by emergent autonomy. One's initial identification with it may be succeeded by disidentification.

Earlier I called attention to the distinction between subjective content that is "ours" in the sense that we experience it, and subjective content that is ours in the deeper sense that we not only experience it but identify with it and act upon it. What emergent autonomy affords is the opportunity to disidentify with aspects of our initially enculturated subjectivity, and this represents the possibility of identifying with an incompossible alternative to it. For a child, to be reared as a Protestant Christian is to be a Protestant Christian; but for an adolescent who exercises his or her emergent autonomy, to have been reared as a Protestant Christian is to pose the question of one's present and future relationship to Protestant Christianity. Implicit in this question is the question of alternatives to that identification.

42

Kierkegaard and Tillich retained their identification with Protestant Christianity and developed it; but autonomy may equally be employed to make and develop an incompossibly alternative self-identification, for example, as an atheist or a Buddhist.

Thoreau's paean to "morning" as the "awakening hour" when "there is least somnolence in us," and his citation from a Chinese sage: "Renew thyself completely each day; do it again, and again, and forever again," is his invitation to live reflectively in awareness of the ever-present opportunity of disidentification.[27] "Renew thyself completely each day" is not understood by Thoreau to mean "transform thyself each day," but to self-awarely renew one's worthy commitments while looking for unworthy traits for the purpose of disidentifying with them. That a person has been a habitual liar, for example, does not seal her future. Thoreau's "morning" theme is the operationalization of Socrates's "examined life."

The effect of the opportunity of self-transformation that autonomy represents is to refute Davidson's thesis that "other minds" can be accessed through the public content of which they are initially the internalization. When persons' autonomy has been exercised to transform this initially enculturated content, their subjectivities can be accessed only through its expressions. Davidson is correct in holding that subjectivity is not a private space accessible only to its owner. When "private" and "public" are defined disjunctively, they are misrepresented, and the same is true of "subjective" and "objective." But the mutual implication of terms in each of these pairs runs not in just one direction but is reciprocal. Enculturation is the subjectivization of objective (public) contents as Davidson contends; but expression is the objectivization of subjective contents—not of the original enculturated subjective contents but of contents that have been transformed by the exercise of autonomy. The poem that begins as a line in one's head moves toward oral or written expression and is incomplete without this. In Emerson's words, "the inmost in due time becomes the outmost."[28] Because it overlooks this reciprocal movement and its intervening autonomy, Davidson's account of the interparticipation of "objective" and "subjective" is one sided.

Davidson, Rorty, Putnam, and Krausz are agreed in holding that human beings have no access to an interpretation-free neutral ground, and I share this thesis; but it does not preclude the exchange of interpretive frameworks that I contend is the work of transcendental imagination. The necessity to knowledge and conduct of *an* interpretive framework is not the inescapability of one's *received* interpretive framework. It was not possible for Whorf (for example) to simultaneously occupy the Hopi perspectival world and his familiar perspectival world, or to view them both *sub specie aeternitatis*, or from a "God's eye" vantage point, but it was possible for him to exchange his familiar world for that of the Hopi.

Against inescapable-received-ethnocentrism John Kekes provides the following, with which I agree.

> The position from which we start . . . is one of unfreedom imposed by our tradition. The imposition is effected by our tradition's providing the language in which we learn to articulate our values, the possible ways of living and acting in terms of which the values can be realized, and the standards by which we evaluate our possibilities.
>
> Moral imagination can overcome these influences through the exercise of its exploratory function. It can acquaint us with possibilities beyond those our tradition provides. It can enlarge the range of possibilities we value. It can also make it possible to reflect critically on the conventional possibilities by comparing and contrasting them with the possibilities we derive from history, ethnography, and literature. As a result we need no longer be restricted to the evaluations conventional standards dictate.
>
> Crucial to understanding the way the exploratory function of moral imagination is connected with freedom is to see that it increases our freedom, rather than makes us free by somehow exempting us from causal influences. If freedom is the absence of coercion and the ability to act according to our values, then moral imagination increases our freedom by allowing us to go beyond the influences of conventional possibilities and standards for evaluating them.
>
> It may be objected to the description of the process just completed that it is misleading to call it an increase of freedom; it is merely an enlargement of the field of causes that exerts its influence upon us. . . . But if we can control what influences us, then this suspicion is misplaced, and moral imagination enables us to control them.[29]

To summarize on inescapable-received-ethnocentrism; as enculturated human beings we indeed can and commonly do interpret the words and conduct of others "by our own lights," but it is not the case that nothing else is possible for us. Such interpretation is a leading cause of the misunderstanding that is endemic in human communication. Because we think we know what the other means by what he or she says and does, we render ourselves impervious to his or her actual meaning as well as to the need to lend ourselves to the other's viewpoint in temporary exchange for our own.

By overcoming the stumbling block of inescapable-received-ethnocentrism, we have cleared the path for further investigation of transcendental imagination, and the next chapter will endeavor to disclose its dynamics by a phenomenological analysis of its occurrences.

Notes

1. Beneath Davidson's argument for the "meaninglessness" of the idea of incommensurable alternative conceptual schemes, which will be treated in this chapter, is his argument for the necessary incoherence of the "very idea" of a conceptual scheme that separates scheme and content. As I will use the notions of "conceptual scheme" and "perspectival world" no such disjunction is implied; scheme and content are inextricably related by mutual implication. In particular I am presupposing that the human mind has no access to "bare (uninterpreted) givens." In N. R. Hanson's terms, all facts are "theory-laden" (*Patterns of Discovery*, Cambridge: Cambridge University Press 1958, p. 19). Davidson is correct that C. I. Lewis dichotomizes scheme and content by employing bare givens in his epistemology, a mistake on Lewis's part that received extended treatment in Israel Scheffler's *Science and Subjectivity* (New York: Bobbs-Merrill, 1967). Given Lewis's avowed pragmatism, it is surprising that he departed from his predecessors in this. It was partly to reject the dichotomy that James developed his "radical empiricism," and to the same purpose Dewey shunned the term "givens" in favor of "takens."

2. Donald Davidson, "The Myth of the Subjective," in *Relativism: Interpretation and Confrontation*, ed. Michael Krausz (Notre Dame: University of Notre Dame Press, 1989), pp. 159–60.

3. Hilary Putnam, *Reason, Truth, and History* (Cambridge: Cambridge University Press, 1981), p. 119.

4. Richard Rorty, "Solidarity or Objectivity?," in Krausz, *Relativism*, p. 40.

5. Michael Krausz, *Rightness and Reasons: Interpretation in Cultural Practices* (Ithaca: Cornell University Press, 1993), pp. 114–15.

6. Davidson, "On the Very Idea of a Conceptual Scheme," in *Relativism, Cognitive and Moral*, ed. Jack W. Meiland and Michael Krausz (Notre Dame: University of Notre Dame Press, 1982), p. 78.

7. Among Quine's discussion of "charity," see Willard Van Orman Quine, *Word and Object* (Cambridge, Mass.: The M.I.T. Press, 1960), pp. 59n, 69n.

8. Davidson, "On the Very Idea of a Conceptual Scheme," in Meiland and Krausz, *Relativism*, p. 78.

9. Alasdair MacIntyre, "Relativism, Power, and Philosophy," in Krausz, *Relativism*, pp. 197–98.

10. Davidson, "The Myth of the Subjective," in Krausz, *Relativism*, p. 160.

11. Ibid.

12. MacIntyre, "Relativism, Power, and Philosophy," in Krausz, *Relativism*, p. 186.

13. Davidson, "On the Very Idea of a Conceptual Scheme," in Meiland and Krausz, *Relativism*, p. 67.

14. Charles S. Peirce, "The Fixation of Belief," in *Selected Writings*, ed. Philip P. Wiener (New York: Dover Publications, 1958), pp. 101–3.

15. Ralph Waldo Emerson, "Self-Reliance," *The Complete Works of Ralph Waldo Emerson* (Boston & New York: Houghton Mifflin, 1903), vol. 2, pp. 81–82.

16. See, e.g., Renate Wilson, *Inside Outward Bound* (Charlotte, N.C.: East Woods Press, 1981).

17. George Santayana, *Scepticism and Animal Faith* (New York: Dover Publications, 1955), p. 11.

18. William James, *Pragmatism*, ed. Bruce Kuklick (Indianapolis: Hackett, 1981), p. 10 ff.

19. Jean-Paul Sartre, *Being and Nothingness*, trans. Hazel E. Barnes (New York: Philosophical Library, 1956), chap. 2, "Bad Faith."

20. Michael Krausz, *Rightness and Reasons* (Ithaca: Cornell University Press, 1993).

21. Ibid. pp. 90–91.

22. Davidson, "The Myth of the Subjective," in Krausz, *Relativism*, p. 166.

23. Ibid., p. 163.

24. Ibid., p. 166.

25. Ibid., p. 171.

26. Soren Kierkegaard, *Fear and Trembling*, trans. Walter Lowrie (Garden City: Doubleday Anchor Books, 1954), p. 80 et seq. Paul Tillich, *The Dynamics of Faith* (New York: Harper Torchbooks, 1958), p. 46.

27. Henry D. Thoreau, *Walden*, ed. J. Lyndom Shanley (Princeton: Princeton University Press, 1971), p. 88.

28. Emerson, "Self-Reliance," *The Collected Works of Ralph Waldo Emerson* (Cambridge: Harvard University Press, 1979), vol. 2, p. 27.

29. John Kekes, *The Morality of Pluralism* (Princeton: Princeton University Press, 1993), p. 114.

Chapter 3

PHENOMENOLOGY OF PERSPECTIVAL EXCHANGE: SHOCK, *GRAVITAS,* AND *LEVITAS*

The experience we speak of as "seeing ourselves through the eyes of another" is attended by a shock of disparity. For example, public performers—actors, musicians, speakers—report that they sometimes suddenly perceive themselves from the viewpoint of a member of their audience. It is disconcerting, because in that perspective they do not know what comes next from the performer. Or as a parent one may on rare occasions suddenly see oneself through the eyes of one's child, appearing as a looming, all-knowing, and powerful presence that ill-accords with one's ordinary self-perception. Or again, while temporarily living abroad, one may perceive one's native land through the eyes of one's hosts—for example, discovering America and Americans in English perspective, or Japanese, or Indian.

49

Shock

The disparity in such cases is between the other's "external" perception of us as an item in his or her world of meanings, and our "internal" perception of ourselves, not as an item, but as the organizing center of our perspectival world. To be sure, we experience occasional shock within our perspectival world; but because that world is a continuum, it is not the shock of irreconcilable disparity but of the unanticipated. It sets the task of subsuming the novelty within our familiar world with, in William James's words, "a minimum of disturbance of the latter."[1] The power of a perspectival world to assimilate novelty of all sorts rests in the fact that events do not come bearing their own meanings but acquire their meanings from human beings. According to C. I. Lewis as cited in chapter 1, "In determining its own interpretations—and only so—the mind legislates for reality, no matter what future experience may bring."[2]

By contrast the shock of disparity blocks the assimilative work of progressively extending the continuum of meanings that constitutes the existing perspectival world. It marks the appearance of an alien possibility, a meaning that, if adhered to, entails an alternative perspectival world. It attests that change in the lives of human beings is of two different sorts, "evolutionary" and "revolutionary." In evolutionary change, the past is preparation for the present and the future. Here shock is contingent, because what was unanticipated was in principle anticipatable, and the disparity that shock registers is merely apparent.

On the other hand, alien possibilities are harbingers of alternative perspectival worlds that are discontinuous with the existing world by virtue of the "closure" of perspectival worlds, which was discussed in chapter 1. Between the existing world and an alien possibility, discontinuity is not merely apparent but real. To *apprehend* an alien possibility is merely to notice an anomaly, perhaps immediately to dismiss it. To *entertain* an alien possibility (in order, in Plato's words, to "determine by reason the meaning of the apparition") constitutes revolutionary exchange of discontinuous perspectives.

C. S. Peirce provides an elemental description of the shock of revolutionary exchange in his essay "The Architecture of Theories."

"Suppose," he says, "I had nothing in my mind but a feeling of blue, which were suddenly to give place to a feeling of red; then, at the instant of transition there would be a shock, a sense of reaction, my blue life being transmitted into red life."[3] The transition is necessarily sudden and total because Peirce is postulating that between the "blue feeling" and the "red feeling" lie no intermediate positions to provide stepping-stones for gradual transition.

For a correlate in our everyday experience, consider the high mood we call elation and the low mood we call depression. There are no stepping-stones between, because each mood bathes the whole of actual and possible experience in its hue. The same happening that yesterday might have contributed to our high spirits is today saturated in the hue of our depression. If yesterday I was overjoyed to receive a substantial raise in salary, today I reflect that "money isn't happiness," that I don't like my job and must now work harder at it, and so on. When one of these moods gives way to the other, the transformation seems to us miraculous and inexplicable.

The shock we speak of is always disconcerting, but by no means always unpleasant. An example of a shock that can be welcome is the "aha!" of illumination attending a gestalt switch, to which Thomas S. Kuhn, for example, initially ascribed a crucial place in the development of scientific knowledge.[4] Moreover, persons who are by disposition adventurous may repeatedly seek out shocks of disparity, for while there is certainly adventure to be found within every perspectival world, especially at its frontiers, the adventure between perspectival worlds is higher keyed, rather more akin to mountaineering than to the quieter day-by-day adventures of, for example, sound child rearing, or working at a good marriage, or writing a book.

Comedy and the "Comedic Vision"

Indeed, the shock of disparity is responsible for comedy, according to such investigators as Kierkegaard, Schopenhauer, Bergson, and Arthur Koestler, where it produces the burst of laughter.

According to Bergson, "A situation is invariably comic when it belongs simultaneously to two altogether independent series of events and is capable of being interpreted in two entirely different meanings at the same time."[5] Similarly, Schopenhauer says, "the phenomenon of laughter always signifies the sudden apprehension of an incongruity" between two incommensurably different appearances of a thing. One of the examples he provides is a tombstone epitaph, "Here he lies like a hero, and those he has slain lie around him," on the grave of a doctor. The reason, Schopenhauer says, that "certain animal forms, such as apes, kangaroos, jumping-hares, etc., sometimes appear to us ludicrous" is that "something about them resembling man leads us to subsume them under the conception of the human form, and starting from this we perceive their incongruity with it."[6]

In the same vein, Arthur Koestler contends that "the pattern underlying all varieties of humor is 'bisociative'—perceiving a situation or event in two habitually incompatible associative contexts. This causes an abrupt transfer of the train of thought from one matrix to another governed by a different logic or 'rule of the game.'" Koestler's term for these dynamics of the comic is "bisociative shock."[7]

It was Kierkegaard who contended that what I call the "bisociative dance" is the appropriate attitude of human beings to their own existence. This is because according to him a human being is an irresolvable paradox of infinite and finite as symbolized by the corporealization of the divine in Christ as Jesus. As this paradox, the human being is strictly unintelligible, and the philosophic quest for self-understanding by means of reason is quixotic. This is Kierkegaard's argument for the requirement of Christian faith.

It is also Kierkegaard's demonstration of the singular appropriateness of the comedic attitude toward human existence. "What lies at the root of both the comic and the tragic . . . is the discrepancy, the contradiction, between the infinite and the finite, the eternal and that which becomes."[8] In the voice of Johannes Climacus, Kierkegaard next explains the difference between the tragic and the comic:

> When [existence is] viewed from a direction looking toward the Idea [the infinite], the apprehension of the discrepancy is pathos; when viewed with the idea behind one, the apprehension is comic. When the subjective existing thinker turns his face toward the Idea, his apprehension of the

discrepancy is pathetic; when he turns his back to the Idea and lets this throw a light from behind over the same discrepancy, the apprehension is in terms of the comic.[9]

Thus, both the tragic and the comic accurately express the inescapable contradiction of human life; but Kierkegaard insists that it is the comic that most authentically reflects the human condition. This is because the comic faces *toward* existence as lit by the idea behind it, while the tragic faces away from existence and toward the idea. The path of the latter, though tragedy itself has but one foot upon it, is that of the thinker, which aims at making existence "tantamount to a thinking about everything." It negates existence by "abstract thought," which is "thought without a thinker."[10] By facing away from its own existence, it is engaged at self-denial, the mark of inauthenticity.

By contrast, comedy faces its existence and lucidly recognizes it as inherently contradictory. But in facing existence, it is not mired in an immanence that is devoid of transcendence because it experiences existence in the light of the infinite. It does not represent the inauthentic, escapist attempt of persons to live in the infinite. Yet it "visits" the infinite intermittently, recognizing it as "where he cannot as an existing subject remain, but only repeatedly arrive."[11] The effect of these visitations is to highlight the paradoxicality of the existence that is to be lived—the disparity between finite and infinite that cannot be resolved or escaped but must be lived, "facing" existence in the comedic dance between its disjunctive aspects.

In the comic dance between finite and infinite, immanent and transcendent, Kierkegaard distinguishes between irony and humor. Irony is focused on particulars, while humor is coextensive with existence, diffused and ubiquitous. Whereas irony perceives finite and infinite in a given thing or situation, humor has a "determinant of totality" that embraces human existence per se.[12] I think an implication of this is that irony and comedy coexist when the interplay of disparate perspectives is upon particular situations that are entirely commonplace, because the commonplace particular possesses the characteristic of generalizing itself: it bespeaks the human condition.

For example: I am in a crowded airport but detached a little from the bustle, observing it from my seat on a bench. Hundreds of people are dashing about, and all of them with bags, boxes, and packs attached to themselves by handles, straps, belts, and cords. Presumably these appendages contain things that the persons cannot do without, and this necessity, so to speak, extends the identity of the persons to include these appendages. It is rather as if the camel's humps were strap-on affairs by which the camel was obliged to extend himself whenever he moved about. This amplified identity is species-specific—only the human animal travels in this "expanded" condition, and I am reminded of Thoreau's lines: "If you are a seer, whenever you meet a man you will see all that he owns, ay, and much that he pretends to disown, behind him, even to his kitchen furniture and all the trumpery which he saves and will not burn, and he will appear to be harnessed to it and making what headway he can."[13] I am also reminded of the update of Thoreau's observation in George Carlin's monologue entitled "Stuff."

Perhaps surprisingly, the centrality of the comic in Kierkegaard is matched by the importance of "the comic vision" in the philosophy of George Santayana. According to Santayana, only "the comic vision" can disrupt two interrelated contaminants of Western thought and Western life that are so prevalent as to warrant the term "normal madness," namely the arrogant anthropocentrism and its attendant "moralism" by which human beings ontologize their comfortable perspectives in order to adduce absolute justification for their lives. According to Santayana, the demand for ontological justification arises from the contingency of existence and serves to falsify the human condition by transforming contingency into metaphysical necessity. In contrast, the comic vision is a coping strategy for living a contingent and inherently insecure existence—Kierkegaard's "authenticity"—with "intellectual humility." "Against evils born of pure vanity and self-deception," Santayana says, and especially "against the verbiage by which man persuades himself that he is the goal and acme of the universe, laughter is the proper defence."[14]

It might be thought that by employing "the infinite" Kierkegaard falls under Santayana's condemnation of "moralism" as described above. But the purpose to which Kierkegaard puts the infinite is not the ontologizing self-justification that Santayana condemns. When the individual faces her existence in the light of the eternal, the effect is to lighten her existence, not to add weight to it as ontologization does. It is for this same effect that Santayana summons the "comic vision."

Another apparent discrepancy is Kierkegaard's insistence upon commitment "in the light of the infinite" to the particularity of one's course of life that is entailed by the individuation of subjects. In contrast, Santayana's temperamental preference for detached contemplation leads him to view committed living with irony. The comic vision, he appears sometimes to say, is the proper province of philosophers, while particularized commitments are what give to human life its tragic aspect. In Santayana's words, "Every one who is sure of his mind, or proud of his office, or anxious about his duty, assumes a tragic mask."[15] In the end, however, philosophers are not exempt. All human beings must inevitably lead particular lives, and commitment to them is not only "the source of [their] troubles," but also "the means to [their] happiness and deliverance."[16]

What Santayana opposes is not commitment by human beings to their particular projects, but the ontologization of those projects by which persons attempt to furnish their own lives with a justification that is, first, spurious, and, second, at cost to persons whose projects are at variance with those that have been ontologized. This obliges him to deal with the purported psychological law, beginning with Plato, but very prevalent in belief today, that human beings will only commit themselves to truths and values that they believe to be absolute and exclusive. Santayana denies the purported law by contending for the compatibility of skepticism and animal faith.

Chapter 4 will provide a case for the psychological compatibility of commitment and pluralism, and argue for the imperative need to shake commitment loose from its absolutist moorings. Commitment must be warrantable because it is a necessary condition of a well-lived life. To detach it from absolutism and connect it with pluralism requires that we replace the questions "What is the truth?" and "What is the summum bonum?" with the question "What truths and values shall I be responsible for?" I believe that commitment in a pluralistic context depends upon and expresses a cardinal virtue (a virtue that is required by all well-lived lives) named "liberality."

Liberality expresses the *sophrosune*—the "proportionality"—of finite lives that acknowledges their finitude.

To the virtue that is exemplified by the conjunction of skepticism and commitment, Santayana gives the name of "chivalry." For him, chivalry is the hallmark of ethical life "from which an intelligent sympathy acknowledges the good of others as *they themselves experience it*."[17] In a paraphrase by Noel O'Sullivan,

> Chivalry is the ability to accept moral and social diversity. It presupposes rejection of the basic human yearning for absolute power. To become chivalrous, that is to say, is to recognize without acrimony that other men are entitled to differ from oneself even on matters most fundamental to one. Thus chivalry does not require any abandonment of one's own interests; it does not aim, as liberalism aims, at the elimination of power from the world; what it does is reject man's tendency to attach absolute significance to those interests.[18]

Recognizing that chivalry is vulnerable to the unmitigated drive for power of what he regards as premoral life, Santayana undertook to describe in *Dominations and Powers* a political society that would both nurture and protect the virtue of chivalry. In *Democracy and Moral Development*, I sought to describe a political society that would cultivate and protect the virtue of liberality.[19] I think there is strong similarity between Santayana's "chivalry" and my "liberality" (both differ from liberal "tolerance," as I show in the next chapter), but I will shortly contend that the route to chivalry as charted by Santayana, namely "ultimate skepticism," cannot be endorsed if we believe that the virtue can and should be widely distributed.

It will be obvious that virtues are outcomes of development if we consider that, for example, wisdom, courage, temperance, and justice are not possessed by children. It is theoretically possible that development is wholly a process of conditioning by which social contents are imprinted in individuals, as unquestionably much childhood development is. But if the whole story of the development of human beings is the internalization of social contents, then human beings are from beginning to end "social products" and totalitarianism—total control of individuals by social agencies—prevails.

I side with the Greek eudaimonists and Santayana in the view that development is the interaction of formative social influences with innate potentialities in individuals; and I democratize innatism by positing that within all normal human beings the potentialities exist for all of the cardinal virtues. Then the pressing question becomes how these potentialities are actualized—a question of method. This theory of agency will be laid out and put to use in chapter 4, but it is logically independent of the theory of transcendental imagination, which it is this book's primary purpose to present.

A foothold on the problem of method for the cultivation of transcendental imagination is afforded by the contrast between the *levitas* of the spirit of comedy, and the *gravitas* of innocent parochialism and everyday life.

Gravitas and *Levitas*

Levitas is the "making light" that attends not only comedy, but also "play," in particular the play of imagination, and the "sportive attitude" that Kant correctly associates with the creativity of genius as distinguished from the creativity of talent. What it lightens is actual existence, both in particulars (as in Kierkegaard's "irony") and in general (as in Kierkegaard's "comedy").

Gravitas is what *levitas* counteracts; it is the inherent weight and seriousness of actuality. At first thought, *gravitas* may appear to be the weight—the inertia and brute resistance—of fact, against which *levitas* is the play of possibilities. But because the existing world is made up not of bare facts but of meaningful facts, it becomes evident that *gravitas* attends not bare facts but the particular meanings of facts in the perspectival world that is presently actual. It attends these meanings because persons who inhabit this perspectival world are identified with them. In Charles Taylor's definition, "We have to think of man as a self-interpreting animal. He is necessarily so, for there is no such thing as the structure of meanings for him independently of his interpretation of them; for one is woven into the other."[20] Here we arrive at the subjective component of *gravitas*; it

57

is the native supposition by human beings that the identities they bear are the only possible identities for them.

The objective correlate is generated by the metaphysical necessity that amid innumerable possibilities, something must exist. Because human beings are meanings-generators, and meanings, to be such, must correlate, what must exist is a meaningful world. Our perspectival world cannot be otherwise than it is if the human beings who inhabit it cannot be otherwise than they are.

It is not by necessity that the world that exists is the presently actual world rather than another, just as it is not by necessity that existing human beings bear their operative identities, rather than some other. Our identities represent the actualization of some possibilities within ourselves when others might have been actualized instead, and facts in the world have possible meanings other than those meanings that are actual.

C. I. Lewis is referring to the subjective component of *gravitas* when he speaks of the "stubborn conservatism of mind."[21] Santayana is referring to its objective component when he says, "Existence itself is a momentary victory of essence: a victory over matter, in that matter, which might have taken any other form, takes this particular form and keeps circling about it, as if fascinated."[22]

In summary, *gravitas* reflects the supposition that what presently is actual is all that is possible—that beyond what presently exists lies nothing. This mistake finds its counterpart in Eastern philosophy in the misconception of Buddhism's *sunyata* and *nirvana* as, respectively, "void" and "extinction" when these are taken in an absolute sense. As the bodhisattva Nagarjuna warns, "Those who cling to the view of 'emptiness only' are incurable!" To imply an image provided by Jizang's commentaries on Nagarjuna, "It is as if the water one were using to extinguish a fire were itself to catch on fire."[23]

What *nirvana* extinguishes is, on one hand the idea of independent, self-subsistent beings, in order to recognize the interdependence of all existence; on the other hand it extinguishes absolute emptiness in order to recognize *sunyata* as potentiality. Together with the actual always is the virtual.

The supposition that beyond existence lies nothing is not, of course, the eradication of possibilities, nor of creativity as the discernment and actualization of possibilities. It is the restriction of the meaning of "possibility" to immanent possibilities, by which creativity is confined to the extrapolation and refinement of the existing world. This is a continuity-theory of existence and human knowledge. American Pragmatism is a conspicuous proponent of continuity-theory, and it will be useful to examine its case.

Continuity and Discontinuity in Knowledge

Peirce advances the thesis of the continuity of knowledge when he says, "No cognition not determined by a previous cognition, then, can be known. It does not exist, then, first, because it is absolutely incognizable, and second, because a cognition only exists so far as it is known."[24] It is obvious that cognitions that are "determined" by previous cognitions will be congruent with them.

Retention by a latter-day Pragmatist of the thesis of continuity of knowledge by virtue of continuity of analysis is evident in the following passage by Israel Scheffler against Thomas Kuhn's scientific "revolutions":

> When one hypothesis is superseded by another, the genuine facts it has purported to account for are not inevitably lost; they are typically passed on to its successor, which conserves them as it reaches out to embrace additional facts. Thus it is that science can be cumulative at the observational or experimental level, despite its lack of cumulativeness at the theoretical level; it strives always, and through varying theories, to save the phenomena while adding to them. And in the case of reduction, a reduced law is itself conserved, *in toto*, as a special consequence of its more general successor. Throughout the apparent flux of changing scientific beliefs, then, there is a solid growth of knowledge which represents progress in empirical understanding. Underlying historical changes of theory, there is, moreover, a constancy of logic and method, which unifies each scientific age with that which preceded it and with that which is yet to follow.[25]

Dewey's insistence on the knowledge continuum is of course legendary. Among countless expressions of the thesis is the following, from *Logic: The Theory of Inquiry*: "The primary postulate of a naturalistic theory of logic is the continuity of the lower (less complex) and the higher (more complex) activities and forms." He adds that the postulate "precludes complete breaks and gaps" in "nature and experience."[26]

A well-known expression of the thesis in the literature of Pragmatism is James's model of knowledge-acquisition.

> New truth is always a go-between, a smoother-over of transitions. It marries old opinion to new fact so as ever to show a minimum of jolt, a maximum of continuity. . . . The individual has a stock of old opinions already, but he meets a new experience that puts them to a strain. Somebody contradicts them; or in a reflective moment he discovers that they contradict each other; or he hears of facts with which they are incompatible; or desires arise in him which they cease to satisfy. The result is an inward trouble to which his mind till then had been a stranger, and from which he seeks to escape by modifying his previous mass of opinions. He saves as much of it as he can, for in this matter of belief we are all extreme conservatives. So he tries to change first this opinion, and then that (for they resist change variously), until at last some new idea comes up which he can graft upon the ancient stock with a minimum of disturbance to the latter, some idea that mediates between the stock and the new experience and runs them into one another most felicitously and expediently.[27]

By the process James describes, the continuum of knowledge is progressively extended and refined. What the process excludes is experience of novelty that *cannot* be "felicitously and expediently" combined with "old opinion" because it is incommensurable with it. This is distinctly odd in James's case, because five years before providing this model, he had not only catalogued abundant examples of incommensurable apprehensions, but had taken them very seriously (see his catalogue of reports of mystical revelations in *Varieties of Religious Experience*). There, James makes it entirely clear that among the characteristics of such apprehensions is that they cannot be "grafted upon" the individual's "stock of old opinions" but are incommensurable with the latter. To be sure, such apprehensions can be dismissed as aberrant, but it is the mark of James's treatment that he does not do this. Instead, he uses the religious experiences he catalogues to support his intuition that "Normal human consciousness is only a narrow extract from a great sea of possible human consciousnesses."[28]

As distinguished from the Pragmatic orthodoxy of James's model of knowledge-acquisition, the side of him that appears in "The Will to Believe," in *Varieties of Religious Experience*, and in his intuition about the constriction of normal human consciousness, displays a hypothetical credulity that is akin to Augustine's *"Credo quia intelligam"*—"Believe, in order to know." It is also akin to Bertrand Russell's advisement, cited in chapter 1, that to understand the viewpoint of another requires "first a kind of hypothetical sympathy, until it is possible to know what it feels like to believe in his theories."

This side of James was too credulous by half for Peirce and Dewey. It entertains the possibility of the "complete breaks and gaps" in experience that Dewey held to be precluded by the "primary postulate of a naturalistic theory of logic." Indeed, it leads in the direction of the "dream metaphysics" that Dewey believed results from taking the phenomenological impressions of shock and immediacy seriously.[29] It is clearly heterdox in respect to Pragmatism if John Herman Randall correctly identifies the cornerstone of that school as the doctrine of the "continuity of analysis."[30]

How the doctrine of the continuity of analysis handles the *appearance* of shock and instantaneity is signally illustrated by Dewey's treatment of "intuition" and "revelation":

> "Intuition" is that meeting of old and new in which the readjustment involved in every form of consciousness is effected suddenly by means of a quick and unexpected harmony which in its bright abruptness is like a flash of revelation; although in fact it is prepared for by long and slow incubation. Oftentimes the union of old and new, of foreground and background, is accomplished by effort, prolonged perhaps to the point of pain. In any case, the background of organized meanings can alone convert the new situation from the obscure into the clear and luminous. When old and new jump together, like sparks when the poles are adjusted, there is intuition. This latter is thus neither an act of pure intellect in apprehending rational truth nor a Crocean grasp by spirit of its own images and states.[31]

Presently, continuity of analysis is relied upon by Richard Rorty to deny the "relativism" of his neo-Pragmatism, as well as by those such as Hilary Putnam who lay the charge. Putnam says, "the whole justification of an interpretive scheme . . . is that it renders the behavior of others at least minimally reasonable by *our* lights," and Rorty agrees with this.[32] In effect, Rorty supposes that we must work from "our lights" because it is all that is possible for us: "We Western liberal intellectuals should accept the fact that we have to start from where we are, and that this means that there are lots of views which we simply cannot take seriously."[33]

The effect of the doctrines of continuity of knowledge and continuity of analysis is to confine understanding to "our lights," where what these lights are is determined by our enculturation in the perspectival world in which our thought and conduct is initially shaped. This is the inescapable-received-ethnocentrism against which we argued in chapter 2. Our access to other lights is afforded by the presence within us of innumerable unactualized possibilities together with those that have been actualized as our lights. Not all experience is additive, as continuity theory would have it; some is transformative, as is attested by the shock of disparity that we have earlier examined. Among transformative experiences must be included our identification with persons whose patterns of belief and conduct are very different from our own.

A Dialectic

To not merely apprehend an incompossible possibility but entertain the world of its compossibles is a dialectical process that Plato describes when he says that a man is not "in his wits" when he attains "prophetic inspiration," but must "recover his wits" in order to understand what has appeared to him. What Plato terms "wits" and what I term "bound consciousness" are applied to the foreign possible in order to explicate its implications, thereby mapping an alternative perspectival world.

This is an altogether different process from "testing" the beliefs of another culture "by trying to weave them together with beliefs we already have."[34] It places understanding before testing in the order of priorities; and following upon understanding the first "test" must be that of determining how well the beliefs and practices of the other culture (or subculture or individual of our own culture whose patterns of thought and conduct differ disjunctively from our own) weave together into an effective life.

An example of the dialectic would be the intuition of the inherent sacredness of the mundane against an antecedent background of dualistic religion. If wits are applied to the intuition, the outcome will be the elaboration of a pantheistic world perspective. In a pantheistic world perspective, the only access to the sacred is through the mundane in which it inheres. (According to Martin Buber, for example, there is no approach to the Thou that is God except through the Thous that are one's fellow human beings.[35]) In a strict dualism, access to God is entirely and exclusively afforded on God's initiative. In the words of Anders Nygren, "there is from man's side no way at all that leads to God. If such a thing as fellowship between God and man nevertheless exists, this can only be due to God's own action; God must Himself come to meet man and offer him His fellowship."[36] Starting from either dualism or pantheism, one cannot get to the other perspective by addition or modification, but only by substitution. Yet pantheism and dualism are not logical contradictories because contradiction is a binary relationship, while such holistic perspectives as pantheism and religious dualism exclude not just one, but multiple, alternatives. In short, incompossibility has broader compass than logical contradiction. Its foundation is Spinoza's "Omnis determinatio est negatio"—all determination is negation.

Another example of the dialectic would be the intuition of one's kinship with the natural world against an antecedent background in which nature was regarded as an adversary to be tamed or as an indifferent pool of resources to be heedlessly exploited. The application of wits to this insight will result in the transformation of everything in the individual's perspectival world in the direction that is presently termed an "ecological" understanding. It is an understanding in which anthropocentric self-aggrandizement and greed are replaced by caring for the natural world, in the senses both of "caring about" and of "tending," as in "caretaking."

Pragmatism deserves great credit for extending and refining the tools by which human beings develop their knowledge of the existing world and improve the quantity of their lives within it. However, the effect of its doctrine of the continuity of analysis is to absolutize the existing perspectival world as the only one possible. In this respect it is a provincialism that cannot meet the present need of humankind to find a ground for the peaceful and productive coexistence of the diverse perspectival worlds that characterize the human presence in the past and the present—in the words of Peter Winch, the "human society, whose very nature is to consist in different and competing ways of life, each offering a different account of the intelligibility of things."[37]

To harmonize this diversity requires abandonment of the ambition to reduce it to identity by the triumph of any one of the perspectival worlds over all others. Our objective must be to discover and implement the ways in which "different accounts of the intelligibility of things" are not competitive but complementary. The first step is to deny legitimacy to the aspiration to dominance of any particular "account of the intelligibility of things," on the ground that the aspiration is invalidated by the finitude and fallibility of human beings. The second step is to be prepared to acknowledge validity in differing accounts—though not any and every account indiscriminately, for pluralism is not the abandonment of criteriology, as I will undertake to show in the next chapter—and this must be personalized as recognition of the validity of systems of belief and patterns of conduct that differ incommensurably from one's own. This requires that the *gravitas* of whatever perspectival world happens to exist be diminished, in order that alternative possibilities be apprehended and entertained, and the worlds they represent be made to disclose themselves by participatory enactment through the exercise of transcendental imagination.

Santayana's "Ultimate Scepticism"

Foreign possibles are not, like Halley's comet, rare visitors to the actual world, but instead continually pelt it in a quiet hail. The

64

reason they for the most part go unperceived is that *gravitas* serves, so to speak, as a protective roof. But anything that works to diminish the *gravitas* of actuality opens perception to the hail of possibilities. In Santayana's philosophy, it is "ultimate skepticism" that does this work. Ultimate skepticism is the conclusion that "nothing given exists," and its effect is to facilitate awareness of the infinite variety of nonexistent givens that Santayana terms "essences." He describes the realm of essence as "the unwritten catalogue, prosaic and infinite, of all the characters possessed by such things as happen to exist, together with the characters which all different things would possess if they existed."[38] Accordingly, "Far from gathering up the fluidity of existence into a few norms for human language and thought to be focused upon, the realm of essence infinitely multiplies that multiplicity, and adds every undiscriminated shade and mode of being to those which man has discriminated or which nature contains."[39]

If our objective is to generalize the availability of transcendental imagination among human beings, ultimate skepticism cannot be the means because it is not reasonable to expect of most persons that they be ready to suspend belief in their own existence. Indeed, Santayana himself affirms that "scepticism is not a life," and represents its attainment as the momentary equipoise of a pendulum at the top of its arc, from which it must in the fraction of an instant descend again.[40] But the attainment will only mark a goal and a triumph for rare individuals who are by disposition as detached and contemplative as Santayana himself. The rarity of the disposition may be judged by the following account of the modality of existence by Santayana: "Existence is accordingly not only doubtful to the sceptic, but odious to the logician. To him it seems a truly monstrous excrescence and superfluity in being, since anything existent is more than the description of it, having suffered an unintelligible emphasis or materialization to fall upon it, which is logically inane and morally comic."[41]

The trouble is that Santayana's essences are a starry but lifeless sky, affording nothing into which vital energies may flow. In contrast, possibilities exert a "pull" that was termed Eros by the ancient Greeks and identified as the living principle of life. When the notion of possibility is substituted for the notion of essence, vital energies are alerted by virtue of the meaning of "possibility" as "possible actuality."

Moreover, ultimate skepticism overshoots the mark, because the *gravitas* of actuality is sufficiently diminished by the disclosure of an alternative to it. Archimedes said that he could move the earth with a lever if only he had somewhere else to stand. The uncovery of so much as a single alternative provides a place to stand, and it opens the door to other alternatives.

The diversity of cotemporaneous cultures in the world includes the coexistence of incommensurable perspectival worlds. In this situation, transcendental imagination can work directly with multiple existences and bypass the skeptical conclusion that "nothing given exists."

MacIntyre's Morphology of Cultures

A different approach to overcoming what I am calling the *gravitas* of whatever perspectival world may be inhabited by a given people is proposed by Alasdair MacIntyre. "What can liberate rationality . . . is precisely an acknowledgement . . . that rationality requires a readiness on our part to accept, and indeed to welcome, a possible defeat of the forms of theory and practice in which it has up till now been taken to be embodied within our own tradition, at the hands of some alien and perhaps as yet largely unintelligible tradition of thought and practice."[42] According to MacIntyre, cultures and traditions are born, wax, wane, and die, and our recognition of the eventual demise of our own culture and tradition renders us sympathetic to alternatives. MacIntyre is relying upon a doctrine known as "morphology" of culture and tradition whose exponents have included Polybius, Machiavelli, Vico, Spengler, Collingwood, and Thomas Kuhn. In MacIntyre's words,

> The development of a problematic within a tradition characteristically goes through certain well-marked stages—not necessarily of course the same stages in every tradition—among them periods in which progress, as judged by the standards internal to that particular tradition, falters or

fails, attempt after attempt to solve or resolve certain key problems or issues is fruitless and the tradition appears, again by its own standards, to have degenerated. Characteristically, if not universally, at this stage contradictions appear that cannot be resolved within the particular tradition's own conceptual framework: that is to say, there can be drawn from within the tradition equally well-grounded support for incompatible positions; at the same time enquiries tend to become diverse and particularized and to lose any overall sense of direction; and debates about realism may become fashionable. And what the adherents of such a tradition may have to learn in such a period is that their tradition lacks the resources to explain its own failing condition. They are all the more likely to learn that if they encounter some other standpoint, conceptually richer and more resourceful, which *is* able to provide just such an explanation.[43]

Leaving aside for now the contentious basic matter of the tenability of cultural morphology, I find several problems in MacIntyre's proposal.[44] One of them is that if the "alien" tradition can successfully resolve *the anomalies in the failing tradition*, this constitutes the commensuration of the two traditions. The upshot is that in a paper expressly devoted to the examination of incommensurable traditions, MacIntyre ends by simply presupposing commensurability. As a related matter, if incommensurability of alternatives obtains, then MacIntyre's characterization of alternative traditions as rivals for supremacy is misrepresentative. In chapter 4, I will argue that the search for a noncompetitive model of relations among alternative cultures and traditions is of vital importance for the world of the twenty-first century.

A second problem has to do with *when* the constituents of a tradition become open to alternative traditions. What MacIntyre relies upon to produce openness is the eventual "failing condition" of one's own tradition as measured by its mounting inability to solve its own problems. To expect anticipation of this eventual failing condition at the time of a tradition's youthful vitality or flourishing maturity is, I think, as unreasonable as to expect a human individual at these stages of his or her life to conduct himself or herself in light of the anticipated debilitation of old age. Moreover, such anticipation could well amount to a counterproductive distraction from the distinctive challenges of his or her present stage. *When* the constituents of a given tradition begin to be receptive to rescue "at the hands of some alien and perhaps even as yet largely unintelligible tradition of thought and practice" is, I think, likely to be at the point at which some evidence of the degeneration of their own tradition is present. But throughout the prior and robust existence of their tradition, it has been situated amid alternative traditions, and I think it is scarcely arguable that cooperative coexistence would be furthered by readiness "to accept, and indeed to welcome" them from the start.

Finally, MacIntyre offers a unilinear model of traditions that succeed one another, with subsequent traditions solving the internal problems of prior traditions. The "liberated rationality" that he calls for is directed entirely to the anticipated tradition that will rescue one's own and succeed it. But one's tradition is all the while situated among alternative traditions that will not in any way solve one's problems, yet contain truths and values of their own. My belief is that a rationality that deserves to be termed "liberated" is one that both can and does recognize and appreciate the intrinsic worth of at least some of these noninstrumental alternatives. In sum, MacIntyre's unlinear model does not address the multilinear situation of multiple traditions.

Developmental Considerations

I have contended that openness to alternatives rests upon the "play" of transcendental imagination, and that this requires a reduction of *gravitas*, which is the grip of an actuality that jealously forbids the entertainment of alternatives to itself. The question I will now address is, "Does *gravitas* sometimes undergo spontaneous diminishment?" which is to say, "Does timing count?" An affirmative answer is implied in Kant's observation regarding what he termed the "productive" imagination by which we "remold experience": "We entertain ourselves with it when experience becomes too commonplace."[45]

The counterpoint to "when experience becomes too commonplace" is to be found in the language of renewal and rebirth that appears in humanistic literature throughout world history. In the morphology of cultures to which reference was made earlier, the history of humankind is represented as renewing itself in the birth of new cultures to succeed old cultures that have outworn their initial inspiration. However, morphology of cultures works (and over-works) an analogy between cultures and individual human lives, and our purpose will be better served by turning to the prototype.

Rebirth and Renewal

The ideas of rebirth and renewal in the lives of individuals finds its home in the conception of the development of individuals as a succession of stages, each with its distinctive developmental requirements. From the ancient sacred literatures of Hinduism and Buddhism, to current developmental psychology, a shared tenet of proponents of this conception is that what diminishes the grip upon persons of the developmental requirements of their current stage, and thereby initiates their receptivity to new requirements, is satisfactory fulfillment of present requirements. The individual may experience a variety of inner and outer inducements to prolong his or her present stage, but when its requirements have been fulfilled, such prolongation becomes perceptibly repetitious, and "experience becomes too commonplace." In this situation transition to the next stage is rebirth to a new developmental world in which one must learn to make one's way. Henry Thoreau is speaking of rebirth to a new stage when he says, "But not until we are lost, in other words, not till we have lost the world do we begin to find ourselves, and realize where we are and the infinite extent of our relations."[46]

In this thesis, *gravitas* spontaneously diminishes at the conclusion of every stage that is successfully negotiated by the individual, preparing him or her for entrance upon the next stage. This applies no less to old age, the final stage of life, where it means that persons who have lived this stage of life well will be less fearful of and resistant to their own death.

In the matter of the systematic cultivation of the capacity for the exercise of transcendental imagination, the appointed time is the onset of adolescence, for which childhood must be an appropriate preparation. This is because adolescence marks the exchange of an identity that has been conferred through the enculturation of dependent childhood for an identity that must be chosen by exercise of the autonomy whose budding announces adolescence's onset. As noted in chapter 1, the threshold of adolescence is marked by the recognition that one or another of the aspects of one's prior child identity no longer fits. This is the invitation to self-identification, and the initial effect of accepting the invitation is, so to speak, to place a question mark beside each of the aspects of the conferred child identity. For example, as a child, to be reared (say) as a Presbyterian; but for an adolescent, to have been reared as a Presbyterian is to pose the question of one's present and future relationship to Presbyterianism. This process of separating from one's conferred child identity may be likened to the loosening of the nut within its shell as it ripens. It can be postponed until later life, as is lately exemplified by large numbers of mature men and women in our society who are struggling to free themselves of their enculturated conception of women. It also can be postponed for a lifetime, in which case the individual lives out the conferred identity of his or her childhood. The developmentally appropriate place for it is adolescence, because the life-shaping choices that lay down one's course in adulthood, deciding one's adult identity and character, are soundly made when they are based not on one's conferred identity but on one's chosen identity.

The process of calling into question the elements of one's conferred child identity is an example of the spontaneous displacement of *gravitas* by *levitas*. By diminishing the weight and seriousness of actuality, it invites the play of possibilities. As noted in chapter 1, what appeared to the child as othernesses that were unrelated to the self, becomes to the adolescent possibilities for the self. Adolescence insistently poses the question, "What would it be like to be this other and that other?"

Adolescent Exploration

Adolescent adventurousness is the exploration of possibilities for the self, and it is a necessary condition of soundness in the life-shaping choices that decide the course of each person's adulthood. As such, it calls for support in a society such as ours that professes to endorse freedom and self-responsibility. Social support would take the form of providing both opportunities for exploration and means for assessing the results that adolescents are unlikely to be able to provide for themselves. It would begin by breaking up our established pattern of schooling as twelve- or sixteen-years-at-one-sitting. It would include internships, apprenticeships, a work-study pattern of education, and a National Service program on lines originally proposed by William James in his 1910 essay, "The Moral Equivalent of War," and subsequently endorsed by Presidents Roosevelt, Kennedy, Johnson, and Clinton, together with many specialists in human development including Margaret Mead, Theodore Hesburgh, Erik Erikson, and James Coleman.[47] In the next chapter I will argue for the centrality of adolescent exploration to a virtue that I believe it has become imperative for human beings to acquire—the virtue of "liberality"—and consider some consequences of our failure to recognize adolescence as a distinctive stage of development with its own inherent and important developmental work to do.

Ex hypothesi, we can exchange perspectives on the world and ourselves because within us are all human possibilities—"Nihil humani a me alienum." But how can we correlate the possibilities we imaginatively actualize with those that constitute the actuality of the particular people or person whom we wish to understand?

Evidence of Correlation

Correlation exists when the beliefs and the conduct of the other make sense on our imaginatively adopted principles of interpretation, not merely in this or that particular, but as a whole. A principle of interpretation that is not the other's may make sense of a few particulars but soon encounters anomalies as we extend it to further particulars. In the apt words of Michael Krausz, the mark of the right interpretive principles is that they "sustain the longer story."[48]

The process of arriving at the interpretation that sustains the

71

longer story is threefold in an analysis by John Kekes that merits extended citation.

> Understanding the significance of particular actions . . . requires the imaginative re-creation of three sets of possibilities: those that were generally available in the agents' context, those that the agents could reasonably be expected to believe themselves to have, and those that the agents actually believed themselves to have.

> This threefold imaginative re-creation of possibilities goes beyond the bare knowledge *that* there were such and such possibilities. To know that much does not require imagination. To understand the significance of particular actions, the attractions, risks, novelty, general regard, emotive connotations, prestige, and so on, associated with the possibilities must be appreciated, and appreciated as they appear to the agents. The understanding of significance, therefore, cannot be merely cognitive, it must also have a large affective component capable of conveying the appeal the relevant possibilities had for the agent. We need a cognitively and affectively informed imagination to re-create the richness of the possibilities whose significance we want to understand. Only against that background does it begin to become understandable why agents realize a particular one among their possibilities.

> Yet the imaginative re-creation of the background is still insufficient for understanding the significance of actions. For there is also the question of the evaluation of the reasons agents give for what they do. The most straightforward situation is when the possibilities the agents actually believe themselves to have coincide with the possibilities reasonable agents would have in that context, and the agents give as their reason that the attraction of the possibility they realized outweighed the attraction of its competitors. In such a case, having re-created the agents' possibilities, we come to appreciate how one of them could have been found to possess greater attraction for the agent than others. And then we could rightly claim to have understood the significance of the particular action.

> But what if we encounter what is so often the case, namely, that some of the beliefs the agents have about their possibilities are in some way unreasonable? It may be that their possibilities are more or less numerous than they believe, or that they find possibilities attractive or unattractive because they ignore readily available features whose acknowledgement would incline them in another direction, or that they are

deceiving themselves, or that their beliefs are misled by anger, fear, fantasy, spite, or envy. In such cases, knowing the reasons the agents give is not enough for understanding the significance of their actions. The search for understanding, then, must go beyond these reasons and explore the question of why there is a discrepancy between what the agents believe about their possibilities and what is reasonable to believe about them. By understanding why the agents are unreasonable, we may come to understand the significance of their actions, even though their significance is hidden from the agents themselves.[49]

On the same page Kekes adds that if this process appears dauntingly difficult, the appearance is deceptive. The kind of understanding it arrives at is regularly achieved by ethnographers, historians, those literary critics "who, unswayed by current destructive practices, still aim to enhance readers' appreciation of the predicaments of fictional characters," and "by all of us in trying to enter sympathetically into the frame of mind of someone we want to know intimately so as to understand the significance of his or her conduct; and by all of us again in the course of the necessary task of trying to make palpable to ourselves what it would be like to realize our possibilities and live according to them so that we may shape our future, if we are reasonable, in as informed a manner as we can achieve."

A Coherence Criterion

That an interpretation shall "sustain the longer story" is a coherence criterion, and as such it encounters two familiar objections. One of them is that coherent systems of ideas may have no existential grounding and, so to speak, hover about the existential world like untethered limp gas balloons. The second objection is that a coherence criterion misrepresents actual persons and peoples by its inability to accommodate the measure of incoherence that actual lives invariably exhibit. Clifford Geertz suggests both objections in holding that

coherence cannot be the major test of validity for a cultural description. Cultural systems must have a minimal degree of coherence, else we would not call them systems; and, by observation, they normally have a great deal more. But there is nothing so coherent as a paranoid's delusion or a swindler's story. The force of our interpretations cannot rest, as they are now so often made to do, on the tightness with which they hold together, or the assurance with which they are argued."[50]

But neither the swindler's story nor the paranoid's can be *lived* coherently: it is because paranoia is dysfunctional that it is categorized as a disease. Thomas Szasz and R. D. Laing have argued that in a dysfunctional world, functionality in individuals is a disease, and such conditions as paranoia represent something like health.[51] In the theory of agency I will offer in chapter 4, health is measured by an individual's success in dealing with the distinctive developmental requirements of each stage of his or her life. Paranoia is dysfunctional because its imaginary problems displace developmental requirements. The swindler's intention is not to live his story but to persuade his victim to live it; however, by attempting to live it the victim falls into a trap and to extricate himself from it requires abandoning the story.

The "untethered gas balloon" objection is similar to G. E. Moore's objections, in "A Defense of Common Sense," to philosophers who by perfectly coherent arguments contradict common sense, for example as J. M. E. McTaggart skillfully and coherently proves the unreality of time. Moore's line of rebuttal is that McTaggart's certainty that nevertheless his morning mail arrived after breakfast attests to the fact that McTaggart himself is unpersuaded by his coherence criterion.[52]

The first objection to the coherence criterion is met by the stipulation that the requisite coherence is not of ideas merely, but also of conduct and feelings, which is to say it is the coherence of a life, whether the life be that of an individual or of a collectivity. That this is not an illegitimate extension of the notion of coherence will be evident if we recognize that whatever appears in human consciousness—material facts, conduct, feelings, ideas—appears as a meaning. In Charles Taylor's observation (cited in Chap. 1), a human being is a "self-interpreting animal. He is necessarily so, for there is no such thing as the structure of meanings for him independently of

74

his interpretation of them; for one is woven into the other." Accordingly, "already to be a living agent is to experience one's situation in terms of certain meanings."

Taylor also provides the appropriate response to the second objection to a coherence criterion that was noted above, and it is twofold. In the first place, he notes that methodological reliance on a coherence criterion "is not to say that all behavior must 'make sense,' if we mean by this be rational, avoid contradiction, confusion of purpose, and the like. Plainly a great deal of our action falls short of this goal. But in another sense, even contradictory, irrational action is 'made sense of' when we understand why it is engaged in. We make sense of an action when there is a coherence between the actions of the agent and the meaning of his situation for him."[53] In short, what we are looking for is the terms in which his action *seemed to him* to make sense. We may recall from chapter 1 similar advice by Bertrand Russell on how to study a text in philosophy: "When an intelligent man expresses a view which seems to us obviously absurd, we should not attempt to prove that it is somehow true, but we should try to understand how it even came to seem true."

The second part of Taylor's answer to the "excessive coherence" criticism is that it belongs to the work of understanding others to surpass the coherence they in fact achieved by envisaging the coherence they sought or are seeking. This rests on the teleological proposition that a person or a culture most essentially is the particular outcome that represents its fulfillment. It leads Taylor to say of the work of understanding another person or culture, "Our aim is to replace this confused, incomplete, partly erroneous self-interpretation by a correct one."[54] Unfortunately, Taylor magnifies the difference between the interpretation and the interpreted. Because the former is "really clearer" than the latter, Taylor holds it to be "out of phase" with it, and says that "the two will not be congruent."[55]

The same idea can be expressed more or less clearly, and so for the same self-interpretation; the differences here are of degree, not of kind. The "not . . . congruent" and "out of phase" pronouncements by Taylor suggest that what he regards as the "correct" self-interpretation is not the clarification of the agent's own self-interpretation, but a substitution provided by the interpreter. This is a mistake on Taylor's part, prompted, I think, by his conviction that the hermeneutical science he advocates, as against the application of the methods and presuppositions of natural science to human conduct, must nevertheless exhibit the detachment that the word "science" connotes to most minds.

It is this allegiance to scientific detachment, together with his insistence that phenomenology is a science, that I think prompts Taylor to reject "the view that misconstrues interpretation as adopting the agent's point of view."[56] Taylor has expressly in mind as the proponent of this view Peter Winch, but the reader will recall from chapter 1 that other proponents include Clifford Geertz, R. G. Collingwood, R. M. Hare, Max Scheler, Martin Buber, and Bertrand Russell.

In order to avoid both what he terms this "incorrigibility thesis" and also the ethnocentrism of imposing upon the explicandum the interpreter's native viewpoint, Taylor proposes to base interpretation as provided by hermeneutical science in "a language of perspicuous contrast." Taylor says, "Such a language of contrast might show their language of understanding to be distorted or inadequate in some respects, or it might show ours to be so (in which case, we might find that understanding them leads to an alteration of our self-understanding, and hence our form of life); or it might show both to be so."[57]

By this move Taylor interposes between "them" and "us" a third standpoint that is neither theirs nor ours. In principle there is nothing wrong with a third standpoint that recognizes itself to be such, but what Taylor's immediate move to it leaves out is the understanding of "their" standpoint *from within*, which is indispensable to the inquiry. If we do not understand the meanings that the phenomena of the experience of a given people have *for them*, we do not understand that people. Lending ourselves to their viewpoint through the exercise of transcendental imagination does not mean capitulating to it, as Taylor's term "incorrigibility thesis" implies. It is normally followed by resumption of our own viewpoint, but it may for comparative purposes be followed by adoption of a third viewpoint (though not as a God's eye, interpretation-free ground). But this is a dialectical process in which the essential first step is "adopting the agent's point of view." In Russell's prescription, "*first* a kind of hypothetical sympathy, until it is possible to know what it feels like to believe in his theories, and only then a revival of the critical attitude, which should resemble, as far as possible, the state of mind of a person abandoning opinions that he has hitherto held" (my emphasis).

Notes

1. William James, *Pragmatism* (New York: New American Library), p. 50.

2. Clarence Irving Lewis, *Mind and the World Order: Outline of a Theory of Knowledge* (New York: Dover Publications, 1956), p. 197.

3. Charles S. Peirce, "The Architecture of Theories," in *Selected Writings*, ed. Philip P. Wiener (New York: Dover Publications, 1958), p. 151.

4. Thomas S. Kuhn, *The Structure of Scientific Revolutions*, 2d ed. (Chicago: University of Chicago Press, 1970), p. 111. Since then Kuhn dropped the reference to gestalt shifts. Responding recently to an interviewer's question, "how would you trace the evolution of your work?," Kuhn says, "I would define it as an increasing emphasis on language, which more and more plays the role that in *Structures of Scientific Revolutions* is played by the Gestalt changes" (in Giovanna Borradori, *The American Philosopher*, trans. Rosanna Crocitto [Chicago: University of Chicago Press, 1994], p. 166). It is my belief that Kuhn's "linguistic turn" leading him to define incommensurability as untranslatability (Borradori, p. 161), harvests for him the intractable problems that I spoke of in connection with Donald Davidson in chapter 2.

5. Henri Bergson, "Laughter," in *Comedy*, ed. Wylie Sypher, (Garden City, N.Y.: Doubleday Anchor Books, 1956), p. 123.

6. Arthur Schopenhauer, *The World as Will and Idea*, trans. R. B. Haldane and J. Kemp (New York: Charles Scribner's Sons, 1883), vol. 2, pp. 271, 273, 279.

7. Arthur Koestler, *The Act of Creation* (New York: Macmillan, 1964), pp. 91, 95.

8. Soren Kierkegaard, *Concluding Unscientific Postscript*, trans. David F. Swenson and Walter Lowrie (Princeton: Princeton University Press, 1941), pp. 82–83.

9. Ibid., p. 83.

10. Ibid., pp. 352, 296.

11. Ibid., p. 75.

12. Ibid., p. 491n.

13. Henry D. Thoreau, *Walden*, ed. J. Lyndon Shanley (Princeton: Princeton University Press, 1971), p. 66.

14. *Little Essays: Drawn from the Writings of George Santayana* (New York: Charles Scribner's Sons, 1920), p. 228.

15. Ibid., pp. 133–34.

16. Paul Arthur Schlipp, *The Philosophy of George Santayana* (Chicago: Open Court, 1940), pp. 12–13.

17. This paraphrase is by Noel O'Sullivan, *Santayana* (St. Albans: Claridge Press, 1992), p. 87.

18. Ibid., pp. 87–88.

19. David L. Norton, *Democracy and Moral Development* (Berkeley: University of California Press, 1991).

20. Charles Taylor, *Philosophy and the Human Sciences* (Cambridge: Cambridge University Press, 1985), p. 26.

21. Clarence Irving Lewis, *Mind and the World Order*, p. 264.

22. George Santayana, *Realms of Being*, one vol. ed. (New York: Charles Scribner's Sons, 1942), p. xiii.

23. Cited in Daisaku Ikeda, *Buddhism, the First Millenium*, trans. Burton Watson (Tokyo & New York: Kodansha International), p. 143. Cited in Alan Fox, "Self-Reflection in the Sanlun Tradition: Madhyamika as the 'Deconstructive Conscience' of Buddhism," *Journal of Chinese Philosophy* 19, no. 1: 8.

24. Charles S. Peirce, "Questions Concerning Certain Faculties," in *Selected Writings*, p. 37.

25. Israel Scheffler, *Science and Subjectivity* (Indianapolis & New York: Bobbs-Merrill, 1967), p. 9. Scheffler is misleading in saying that "genuine facts" are not lost when one scientific hypothesis succeeds another. Some of what were genuine facts under the predecessor hypothesis drop out as no longer such under the successor hypothesis, as Ptolemaic epicycles dropped out of the heliocentric conception of our planetary system, and phlogiston dropped out of the oxygenation theory of combustion. Facts that are retained are transformed in meaning. He is also misleading when he says "a reduced law is conserved *en toto* as a special consequence of its more general successor." The point is that its reduction is a transformation in its meaning. For example, Newtonian mechanics is retained in the Einsteinian universe as an approximately correct description within the parameters of middle-sized objects, terrestrial distances, and moderate velocities. But this is very different from what Newtonian mechanics was believed to be prior to Einstein.

26. John Dewey, *Logic: The Theory of Inquiry* (New York: Henry Holt, 1938), p. 23.

27. James, *Pragmatism*, pp. 51, 50.

28. William James, *The Will to Believe and Other Essays in Popular Philos-*

ophy, ed. Frederick H. Burkhart, Fredson Bowers, and Ignas K. Skrupskells (Cambridge: Harvard University Press, 1979), appendix 4, p. 438.

29. John Dewey, *Art as Experience* (New York: Capricorn Books, 1958), p. 293.

30. John Herman Randall, Jr., "The Nature of Naturalism," in *Naturalism and the Human Spirit* ed. Y. H. Krikorian, (New York: 1959), p. 356.

31. Dewey, *Art as Experience*, p. 266.

32. Cited in Richard Rorty, "Solidarity or Objectivity?," in *Relativism: Interpretation and Confrontation*, ed. Michael Krausz (Notre Dame: University of Notre Dame Press, 1989), p. 39.

33. Ibid., p. 44.

34. Ibid., p. 40.

35. Martin Buber, *I and Thou*, trans. Walter Kaufmann (New York: Charles Scribner's Sons, 1970), Third Part, e.g., p. 123: "Through every single You the basic word addresses the eternal You."

36. Anders Nygren, *Agape and Eros*, trans. Philip S. Watson (Philadelphia: Westminister Press, 1953), p. 80.

37. Peter Winch, *The Idea of a Social Science and Its Relation to Philosophy* (London: Routledge & Kegan Paul, 1950), p. 103.

38. George Santayana, *Scepticism and Animal Faith* (New York: Dover Publications, 1955), p. 77. The phrase is the title of chapter 7.

39. Ibid., p. 78.

40. Ibid., pp. 69, 107.

41. Ibid., p. 48.

42. Alasdair MacIntyre, "Relativism, Power, and Philosophy," in Krausz *Relativism*, pp. 201–2.

43. Ibid., p. 200.

44. Most of the trouble with the morphological thesis comes from drawing the analogy between the life of a culture and the life of an individual (the prototype) too closely, with failure to note where the analogy ceases to hold. A conspicuous case is those morphologists who take the succession of stages in the life of a culture, from its childhood to its decline and death, as an iron law. Oswald Spengler in his *Decline of the West* is an example. But from the necessary death of individuals does not follow the necessary decline and death of cultures. The reason is that by encompassing succeeding generations of human beings, cultures include waves of new energy by which they may revitalize themselves—or they may not. The crucial determinant in whether or not they reenergize themselves is whether or not they can accommodate the *originality* in each new generation that accompanies the energy. A vital tradition is conservative on its trailing edge but exploratory at its leading edge. Where exploration

of new possibilities is stifled by institutionalized orthodoxy, the tradition degenerates into dead usages until finally the mold must be broken.

45. Immanuel Kant, *The Critique of Judgment*, trans. James Creed Meredith (Oxford: Oxford University Press, 1952), p. 176.

46. Thoreau, *Walden*, p. 171.

47. Norton, *Democracy and Moral Development*, ch. 3.

48. In conversation.

49. John Kekes, *The Morality of Pluralism* (Princeton: Princeton University Press, 1993), pp. 102–4.

50. Clifford Geertz, *The Interpretation of Cultures* (New York: Basic Books, 1973), pp. 17–18.

51. The thesis is foundational to most if not all of the work of Szasz and Laing, for example: Thomas Szasz, *The Myth of Mental Illness: Foundations of a Theory of Personal Conduct*, rev. ed. (New York: Harper & Row, 1974). And R. D. Laing and A. Esterson, *Sanity, Madness, and the Family* (London: Tavistock Publications, 1964), e.g., Introduction.

52. Vere Chapell, "Malcolm on Moore," *Mind*, 70, no. 279 (July 1961): 420–21. G. E. Moore, "A Defense of Common Sense," *Contemporary British Philosophy* 2 (1925): pp. 193–223.

53. Taylor, *Philosophy and the Human Sciences*, p. 24.

54. Ibid., p. 26.

55. Ibid., p. 27.

56. Ibid., p. 123.

57. Ibid., pp. 125–26.

Chapter 4

BEYOND TOLERANCE: MULTIPLISM, COMMITMENT, AND THE VIRTUE OF LIBERALITY

By the virtue of "liberality" I refer to the cultivated disposition to recognize and appreciate truths and values other than one's own. The primary thesis of previous chapters is that where others' truths and values are incommensurable with our own, recognition and appreciation of them as the truths and values they represent require that we lend ourselves to the viewpoint of those whose truths and values they are—we exchange our perspectival world for theirs—by the exercise of transcendental imagination. This does not preclude criticism of others' truths and values, either by standards internal to their perspectival world or by such external standards as their compatibility with alternative truths and values, which it is a purpose of this chapter to delineate.

The main purpose of this chapter is to present and defend the thesis that the virtue of liberality is essential to the human sensibility that changing conditions in the world require. As an important corollary I must show that the virtue of liberality does not produce "root-less cosmopolitanism" by eradicating rational justification for partic-ularized commitments by individuals and groups.

Liberality and Global Human Problems

The striking characteristic of many of the problems that presently imperil human beings—war and terrorism, hunger, overpopulation, depletion of natural resources, environmental destruction, currency instability, trade imbalance—is that they are global in scope and will require worldwide cooperation if they are to be promisingly ad-dressed. This points toward limited world federation as an essential condition of human welfare in the twenty-first century. The cooper-ative interaction that is thus mandated requires the abandonment of insular notions of absolute national sovereignty and of an "atomic" core of individuality that is independent of social relations. Such cooperation depends for its stability upon the recognition by nations, peoples, and individuals of the distinctive worth of the contributions by other nations, peoples, and individuals. Merely formal or diplo-matic recognition will not serve, because it can effectively cloak an aspiration to dominance that is biding its time, and this aspiration belongs to the sensibility that must be supplanted. The supplanting sensibility rests in an appreciation of diversity that must be substan-tive, and for it to be such requires experience of the perspectival worlds in which various alternative sets of truths and values are the operative truths and values. Such experience is gained by ex-changing our "home" perspectival world for alternative perspectival worlds through the exercise of transcendental imagination.

Dogmatic Absolutism

In the realm of thought and belief, the great enemy of a stable and appreciatively interactive diversity is dogmatic absolutism, by which I mean the claims of peoples, parties, and individuals to exclusive possession of the whole of ultimate truth and value. By a deep irony, the increasingly evident need for worldwide cooperation on exigent global problems is paralleled by the resurgence of dogmatic absolutism. In the form of religious fundamentalisms, militant nationalisms, and vengeful ethnicisms, this resurgence holds prospect of pandemic balkanization, pitting nation against nation, religion against religion, and race against race.

The explosive charge in dogmatic absolutism is the hostility it provokes by denigrating every alternative to itself as false, misguided, perverse, or evil. Currently the balkanization that is being produced by rival dogmatic absolutisms displays the prospect of monumentally increased human suffering, both in the raw terms of persecution and bloodshed, and also by the intensification of the above-noted global exigencies, as symbolized by the burning Kuwaiti oil fields during and after the Persian Gulf War.

What is needed in the realm of thought and belief is a root-and-branch discrediting of dogmatic absolutism, and more generally a severance of the conceptual and psychological linkage of the notion of exclusivity to claims to the possession of truth and value. I intend to show that in regard to the types of truth and value to which dogmatic absolutisms lay claim, exclusive possession of the ultimate truth is precluded by the aspectual character of the questions. This means that, in regard to such questions, the warranted aspiration of finite individuals and groups is not to the possession of the whole but to aspects of truth and value. Nonexclusivity means that good reasons for the beliefs and patterns of conduct of a people or a person do not preclude the possibility that alternative beliefs and patterns of conduct are likewise supportable by good reasons.

Epistemic Multiplism

Epistemic multiplism is an epistemological condition that is termed "multiplism" by Michael Krausz, and the model I propose for it is that of a division of labor with respect to the realization of truth and value. If the notion of "ultimate truth" is retained, it is in the form of a composite. The ultimate truth about anything is the composite of alternative aspects of truth about that thing, as disclosed and complementary alternative valid perspectives upon that thing. Accordingly the pursuit of ultimate truth is inherently a cooperative enterprise. Complementarity provides the basis for cooperation among entities to which common ground is precluded by incommensurability. It exists among alternative perspectival worlds when the betterment of each contributes indirectly to the betterment of others, or at minimum does not detract from others' betterment. For example, the distinctive "American experience" contributes uniquely to the self-understanding of humankind, and thereby to the self-understanding of every human being and likewise for the distinctive "Japanese experience," the distinctive "French experience," the distinctive "Hopi experience," and so on. Each culture and tradition stands to learn from others of possibilities that are lacking in its own guiding ideal of complete humanness, in some cases to its detriment.[1] Incommensurability precludes direct importation, but a home culture may consider whether its guiding ideal can be improved by the introduction in its own terms of a counterpart. For example, do we in twentieth-century United States suffer from lack of a counterpart to Hellenic Greek *eudaimonia*, or the *amor fati* of Republican Rome, or tribal veneration of elders, or the pantheistic understanding of the kinship of all being?

To be sure, in any interactive multiplicity conflicts will arise. What the presence of complementarity in the model provides is the direction in which conflict resolution is to be sought, which provides guidance in the selection of appropriate means.

The epistemic ideal of which multiplism is the antithesis is termed "singularism" by Krausz, and his demonstration in *Rightness and Reasons* that multiplism is the epistemic condition of certain questions is intended to refute the thesis that singularism is "the sine qua non of rationality."[2] Krausz exhibits exemplary scrupulosity by confining his claims for multiplism to the examples he analyzes, and concluding with the suggestion that the terms and strategies he provides may be extended "on a piecemeal basis" to a wider range of questions.[3] In this way he ensures that the reach of *Rightness and Reasons* never exceeds its grasp. My own ambition for this work is larger, for I hope to show that the multiplism he demonstrates is a definitive condition of all cultural objects-of-interpretation by any

84

viable meaning of "culture," and that it discredits dogmatic absolut-ism. The fulcrum of my argument will be a class of propositions that I will term "directional" because they provide answers to the directional question that is posed by the inherent problematicity of human being—"What kind of life shall be lived?" Dogmatic abso-lutisms invariably center in directional propositions because they en-deavor to control human lives. Cultures center in directional proposi-tions because they must direct the growth of successive generations of their young by processes of enculturation. My intention is to show by extrapolation of Krausz's presentation that the epistemic condi-tion of directional propositions is multiplist.

Thereafter I will offer a rebuttal of the charge that multiplism erodes the ground of particular commitments by individuals and groups, and conclude by showing the requirement to supplant "tol-erance" by the virtue of liberality as the means for the peaceable and productive accommodation of diversity. But now to *Rightness and Reasons*.

Global singularism is defined by Krausz as the thesis that for any object of interpretation there can be one and only one ideally right interpretation, where "right" is used in the bipolar sense according to which every alternative to the right interpretation must be "wrong." In contrast, multiplism is a different ideal of interpretation. It obtains in cases of objects of interpretation for which "admissible" (the term Krausz uses to avoid the implied exclusivity of "right") interpretations cannot ideally be reduced to one. Krausz does not contend that there are no objects of interpretation that answer to singularism, which is to say that his multiplist thesis is not global. Rather, his contention is that whether the condition of singularism or of multiplism applies to a given object of interpretation must be determined on a piecemeal basis by analysis of specific cases.

Multiplism applies when to a question there is more than one interpretation that is backed by good supporting reasons, yet the reasons are "inconclusive" in the sense that they cannot preclude other interpretations for which good supporting reasons can be pro-vided. They cannot be conclusive because of the absence of neutral overarching standards by which to rank relative to one another the supporting reasons for alternative interpretations. Absence of neutral overarching standards identifies alternative interpretations as "incommensurable" in the definition of this term that Krausz draws from mathematics.[4]

The examples for which Krausz provides detailed analyses are of "cultural" objects-of-interpretation—objects that must be understood in terms of the practices that produce them. He leaves open the question of whether mathematics, formal logics, and the natural sciences are cultural practices in this sense. His chosen examples are musical scores, paintings, poems, face-or-vase figures (focussing the issue of imputationalism and anti-imputationalism in interpretation), historical interpretations, cross-cultural interpretations, and self-interpretations. For purposes of my above-indicated generalization, any of Krausz's analyses will serve, and my choice will be his treatment of musical scores. Turning to the issue of commitment, I will draw from Krausz on self-interpretation, but supplement his case for multiplism with a logically independent case of my own in behalf of an innatist thesis that I will defend against the currently prevalent "social constructionist" theory of the formation of the self.

Multiplism in Musical Interpretation: An Example

Krausz devotes the opening chapter of *Rightness and Reasons* to the tradition of orchestral music. A definitive characteristic of that tradition is that a composer's scores underdetermine performances of them and thereby require interpretation; and scores likewise underdetermine their interpretation, from which it follows that interpretations will be multiple. To be "admissible," interpretations must be such that good reasons can be provided for them; and admissible interpretations will be irreducible if no neutral overarching standards exist by which to adjudicate among the justifying reasons that qualify various interpretations as admissible. Finally, multiplism will be established as the applicable epistemic ideal if it can conclusively be demonstrated that in regard to the interpretation of orchestral scores the existence of neutral overarching standards is impossible.

If we take the score of a Beethoven symphony as an example, multiplicity of admissible interpretations is illustrated by such alternative versions as those of Toscanini, Stokowski, Walter, Beecham, Ormandy, and Muti. To suppose that one of these interpretations is "right" in the bipolar sense in which others must be "wrong" is a conceptual mistake, because we possess no neutral and inclusively applicable standards by which to support such a judgment. This absence of a common standard signifies the incommensurability of alternative admissible interpretations according to the definition of "incommensurability" as absence of such a standard.

Incommensurability of score interpretations receives several detailed illustrations by Krausz. One of them centers in a portion of the first movement of Beethoven's First Symphony that by its scoring necessitates a disjunctive choice between the interpretive principles of fidelity to the score or of aesthetic consistency. In Krausz's words,

> Good reasons have been given for performing the passage either way. . . . Despite the fact that the overwhelming tendency is to favor the principle of aesthetic consistency, neither is *conclusively* right. . . . [T]o make the principle of faithfulness to the score subservient to the principle of aesthetic consistency, or vice versa, would require some overarching standard to effect such conclusive ranking. But none is available. Consequently, affirming one interpretation as ideally admissible does not exclude the other as ideally admissible. This amounts to a case of multiplism.[5]

Another example of incommensurability provided by Krausz is the contrast between the usual practice of playing Beethoven's symphonies on modern instruments, and Roger Norrington's reliance on the period instruments that were available to Beethoven. Norrington's aim is fidelity to the sound that Beethoven achieved. In contrast, Riccardo Muti contends that modern instruments would have been welcomed by Beethoven as better able to realize the effects he sought. Again, Krausz observes that both approaches are admissible by virtue of the good reasons for each, while neither interpretation denies admissibility to the other because there are no neutral or common standards to support such a judgment.[6]

As yet another example, the lavish sound of Ormandy and the restrained sound of Fritz Reiner are incommensurables. Both are permitted by the score of a Beethoven symphony as well as by the inherent versatility of the musical instruments for which it is orchestrated.

Here as in each of his examples of multiplism, Krausz scrupulously anticipates possible singularist counterarguments and endeavors to present the best case for each. Among singularist rejoinders that receive detailed treatment are the following claims: that ideally scores should fully determine their interpretations; that fuller determination can be arrived at by supplementing scores with other indicators of composers' intentions; that fuller determination can be achieved by postulating a determinate composer; that a fully determinate "musical work" underlies the score and must be uncovered; and that multiple interpretations pluralize their object-of-interpretation such that each is the singularly right interpretation of its distinctive object.[7]

Krausz provides specific rebuttals of two basic kinds: either the singularist resorts to something that is even less capable of fully determining its own singularly right interpretation than the musical score (an underlying and unscored "musical work" or a plurality of them; a composer's expressions of his intentions in words), or else the strategy amounts to begging the question (the postulated fully determinate composer).

To establish multiplism as an alternative ideal, arguments are needed to show not just that neutral standards by which to judge alternative interpretations do not exist, but that it is impossible that they shall ever be found. To this effect the arguments provided by Krausz are two: that any set of standards is necessarily embedded in a viewpoint that as such cannot be neutral with respect to itself[8]; and that the ideal of singularism misrepresents the nature of orchestral music as defined by its tradition. In consequence, if, for example, singularism were to be the appropriate interpretive ideal in regard to computer music, the proper conclusion would be that computer music launches a new tradition.[9]

Krausz achieves exceptional clarity of focus upon the multiplism-singularism issue by demonstrating that it is logically independent of two other issues with which it is commonly intermixed, namely, imputationalism versus anti-imputationalism in theory of interpretation, and ontological realism versus ontological constructionism. He shows that imputationalism and anti-imputationalism are consistent with either singularism or multiplism, and the same is the case for both ontological realism and ontological constructionism.[10] Since neither singularism nor multiplism entails or presupposes one side or the other in respect to either of these two issues, its logical independence of them is established. But I will not summarize these ground-clearing arguments by Krausz, in order to pursue a question Krausz raises at the conclusion of his study but leaves open, namely, "to what extent singularism and multiplism might distinguish the cultural from the noncultural realms."[11] My intention is to show that on any viable meaning of the term, "culture" entails multiplism, and therefore that multiplism is the epistemic condition of all objects-of-interpretation that are properly termed "cultural."

Generalization: Culture as Multiplist

Biologically, "culture" means "cultivated growth," and this meaning is retained in the anthropological and sociological significations of the term, but with the added features that the growth in question is of a human collectivity, that it in some manner unites successive generations and is therefore a tradition, and that it is in important respects cumulative. To be cumulative, the growth of a culture must incorporate the originality of successive generations, and this is the source of cultural vitality. Without infusions of orginality from its new generations, a culture degenerates into empty usages from which historians must reconstruct what the living culture once was.

As a tradition a living culture must be conservative at its trailing edge, but exploratory at its leading edge. It must preserve in some recognizable form the operative values of its past, but it must also explore new possibilities and entertain them as candidates for inclusion in its matrix. Because culture is centrally a semiotic enterprise, such possibilities are new meanings whose inclusion in the matrix is not independent of the conserved values, but discloses new aspects of their meaning and thereby preserves their vitality as living values. It follows that whatever constitutes an object-of-interpretation in a living culture, beginning with its conserved values, must be perpetually susceptible of disclosure of new aspects of its meaning in the light of fresh perspectives that are the response of new generations to changing circumstances. This is the epistemic condition of multiplism; and to apply singularism to cultural objects-of-interpretation is advertently or inadvertently to aim at transforming a living culture into a lifeless museum piece.

Nor is singularism the appropriate ideal of interpretation in regard to dead cultures, for the historian's task is to bring them to life again by recovering events within them as crossroads of the dialectic of alternative interpretations of them by those who participated in them or were affected by them. The singularism that is implicit, for example, in the contention by Patrick Nowell-Smith that the historian's task is to recover "the only past there was" is a mortician's prescription.[12]

To state my thesis in the negative: whatever is not susceptible of irreducibly multiple alternative admissible interpretations is not a cultural object-of-interpretation. For example, if Shakespeare had successfully limited the admissible interpretations of *Hamlet* to one, then *Hamlet* would not be a cultural object-of-interpretation. If objects of inquiry in the physical sciences are properly classed as cultural, it is because they are susceptible of alternative admissible interpretations, as Thomas Kuhn has famously argued in his contention for multiple paradigms of interpretation.

The example of Shakespeare is counterfactual, but instances are not uncommon of contributors to culture—especially founders of schools of thought or of practices—who attempt to police the interpretations of their contributions, thereby to create abject discipleship in their followers by extinguishing originality of interpretation. The spectacle has about it something pathetic, something discordant, and something odious. It is pathetic because it is certain to fail; it is discordant because it is at odds with what I have just argued is the room for innovative interpretation that a living culture must provide; and it is odious because it violates the principle that persons are to be treated as ends in themselves and never merely as means. In effect, to contribute to culture is an act of trust because it is an invitation to the originality of interpretation of succeeding generations. In the Bedouin motto of the North African desert, "Drink at the well, and give your place to another."

Returning to dogmatic absolutism, it can be decisively discredited if it can be shown that central to the various forms of it are singularist answers to a type of question that represents the epistemic condition of multiplism. In short, dogmatic absolutisms rest upon a category mistake.

To be sure, singularism is not dogmatic absolutism, and a singularist can in self-consistency rebut the particular exclusivist truth-claims of particular dogmatic absolutists on a case-by-case basis. Because singularism endorses exclusivism in its ideal, a dogmatic absolutism can accommodate to the demonstration that it does not *possess* the final and exclusive truth by claiming that it is on the exclusively right path. This claim is consistent in principle with even the "fallibilist absolutism" of Karl Popper and its counterpart in the "limit-concept of ideal truth" of Hilary Putnam. In Popper's words, "One great advantage of the theory of objective or absolute truth is that it allows us to say—with Xenophanes—that we search for truth, but may not know it when we have found it; that we have no criterion of truth, but are nevertheless guided by the idea of truth as a regulative principle."[13]

"Regulative principle" singularists characteristically hold that singularity in the ideal of ultimate truth is a necessary condition for the meaningfulness of the idea of progress, but this makes the unwarranted presupposition that progress must be unilinear. In Krausz's words, Popper's

> method of error elimination [his method of progress] still applies if one allows that the range of ideally admissible interpretations is not singular. Singularism is no requirement for the idea of growth. The ideal results of error elimination need not be the conclusive overthrow of all but one competing interpretation. Put otherwise, the multiplist allows that state Q would be progressive over state P if Q more nearly approximates either X, Y, or Z—these latter states in turn not being conclusively rankable.[14]

"Directional" Questions

The reason that human cultures in the world and the dogmatic absolutisms that balkanize the world exhibit the epistemological condi-

91

tion of multiplism has been noted previously. It is that to be what they are, they must provide answers to the question, "What direction shall human lives take?," and the question is multiplist. Good reasons can be provided for alternative answers, but no such reasons can be conclusive in the sense of precluding admissible alternatives because there are no neutral overarching criteria by which to support conclusively. Accordingly, what is meant by a "culture" is conceptually divorced from dogmatic absolutism. We will shortly take up the question of whether it can be psychologically divorced from absolutism, which is to say: Is conviction of the exclusive truth of one's beliefs a necessary condition of resolute commitment to them and to the life that represents the enactment of them?

Priority of the question, "What direction shall human life (our life, my life) take?" arises from the inherent problematicity of human being. Thanks to metaphysical and biological underdetermination, to be a human being is at bottom to be a twofold problem to oneself, namely the problem of deciding what kind of person to become and the problem of endeavoring to become it.

If I am introducing essentialism here, I believe it to be of a benign form. The essentialism lies in my contention for a universal and definitive characteristic of human beings that is logically prior to culture. I call this characteristic the "problematicity of human being," and it sets for all cultures the task of providing shape to the lives that are lived within them. But as an "essence" problematicity is not *presence* but *lack*, and what in the first instance ministers to the lack is the variable of enculturation. Accordingly, "what we essentially are" cannot be used to legislate cultural diversity away or to minimize its importance. To put the matter in another way, the essentialism here is in the form of a question that must be answered, but answers will be irreducibly multiple and historicized. In contrast to classical essentialism, which claimed perfect and final knowledge of entities by the purportedly infallible intellectual intuition of their essences, answers to the problematicity of human being can only be known and judged a posteriori. The effect of classical essentialism was to put an end to inquiry, but the effect of problematicity is to endorse ongoing inquiry and experimentation.

It is inevitable that the initial shaping of human lives shall occur

through processes of enculturation because human beings are neotenus—born in an embryonic condition and destined to a long dependency. Thanks to dependence, identity formation in childhood in
terms of beliefs, feelings, conduct, and self-conceptions can only
occur through internalization by children of socially established patterns. In a totalitarian society, enculturation is a conditioning that is
designed to determine the specific direction that subsequent growth
will take, but in what is termed a free society enculturation lays out
a range of acceptable possibilities for the direction of subsequent
growth. Whereas a totalitarian society seeks to extinguish the role of
individual choice in the processes of self-formation, a free society
expects that the initial stage of formation of the self by social agencies will be succeeded by each individual's self-formation initiated
by his or her choice among the range of socially endorsed possibilities
for subsequent growth; and the initial social formation of the self
must be designed to equip persons with the resources that subsequent self-determination will require.

The universal answer to the question, "What direction shall
human life take?," is "The direction of truth and value." But truths
and values lie in innumerable directions, and for a finite entity to
pursue them all is as impossible as it is to move in every direction at
once. Accordingly, the directional question for a culture is, "For
which truths and values shall we as a people hold ourselves responsible?," and the directional question for an individual is, "For which
truths and values shall I hold myself responsible?" Because inherent
in the meaning of truth and value are good reasons for the pursuit
of them, to declare oneself for particular truths and values entails
acknowledgment of admissible alternative courses of life in the service of other truths and values.

The case of the individual is epitomized by my situation, as I
write, in my office on the campus of a university. I am surrounded
by colleges and departments each of which bears responsibility for
tending to truths and values in its domain. Thus, there are truths in
the care of the department of English, the department of history, the
college of nursing, the college of agriculture, the college of engineer-
ing, and so on. But the truths and values for which I bear and accept
responsibility fall within the purview of the department of philoso-

93

phy, and I could no more assume responsibility for the truths and values of other departments than I can lead all lives. I say to others, "I wish you well; and I hope to hear from you from time to time about the truths and values that you serve; but to serve them is your responsibility, while my responsibility lies elsewhere."

To be sure, in my university as in every other there are some shared truths and values; but they can be served only in the concrete ways that are established by the particular commitments that are represented by the various colleges and departments. My good reasons for endeavoring to serve the truths and values that I do endeavor to serve are matched by others' comparable good reasons for their alternative service.

The situation I have just described is analogous in key respects to the situation of finite cultures. In order to live and move, they require a direction, and that direction, in order to serve truth and value, can only be established by serving certain truths and values to the neglect of others.

Commitment

We have now arrived at the necessity of particularity in the commitments of finite entities in order to establish direction as required by the problematicity of human being, and the question that calls for attention is, How does multiplism bear upon this necessity? The possibilities appear to be two: either admissibility places the admitted options on an equal footing in relation to the particular entity (culture, person), or it retains the possibility that for each particular entity there is a particular best among the admissible options. If the latter, the good reasons in support of a particular option for a particular culture or person must be different in kind from the good reasons that account for the admissibility of each of the admissible multiple options, because by the meaning of multiplism these cannot be specific to just one culture or person.

To revert to the example of my situation on a university campus: there are good reasons for the pursuit of scholarship and the conduct of teaching in each of the disciplines that are represented by all of

94

the included colleges and departments. Does this mean that for each particular individual it would be just as good to engage himself or herself at any one of them—just as good for me, for example, to be a historian or a mathematician or an entomologist as to be a philosopher? This certainly does not seem to me to be the case. There are some disciplines toward which I find the idea of their work as my work unattractive, yet with no least doubt on my part of their importance. And there are no other disciplines toward which I am drawn by the magnetisim that attracts me to philosophy, a magnetism that I experience as a curious kind of necessity. I now want to show that multiplism accommodates the person-specific relationship that is marked by this kind of necessity, and that the conditions for the discovery of the relationship are universal among human beings.

Consider the case of muliplism in musical interpretation as presented by Krausz. If Riccardo Muti, for example, is a multiplist, we may expect that he will endorse a number of interpretations of a given Beethoven symphony—let us say Toscanini's, Walter's, and Ormandy's. But I think he will be endorsing Toscanini's *as Toscanini's*, Walter's *as Walter's*, and Ormandy's *as Ormandy's*. At the same time what will satisfy him as his own best interpretation is different from theirs, and he is drawn to it by a personal connection to that interpretation alone, as is indicated by his endorsement of others' interpretations as *theirs*. This is entirely consistent with multiplism so long as no attempt is made to conflate the various admissible interpretations.

To approach my thesis of the universalizability of person-specific moral necessity, I will now enlarge the setting. In a free society the self-determination that follows upon the initial social formation of selves in the dependent first stage of life occurs by means of a number of life-shaping choices. These include choice of vocation; choice of whether to marry or not, and whom; choice of whether to have children or not, and how many, and when; choice of vocations; of friendships to cultivate, of locale of permanent residence (or vagabondage); and of civic and religious commitments. Each of these choices establishes a direction of development, and in order that the life in question be lived effectively and the identity of the individual be formed, the separate strands represented by the enactment of

95

each of the life-shaping choices must be integrated. They are integrated when furtherance of each of them contributes to, or at minimum does not detract from, furtherance of the others. This is a condition that we term "integrity." The not uncommon condition in which various of the strands in the life of the individual are in conflict with one another (marriage with vocation, religious beliefs with weekday conduct, etc.) is a condition of inner strife that obstructs worthy living.

As in the case of multiplism in musical interpretation, so likewise in this context, person-specificity of best answers is compatible with multiplism. For each of the questions that is answered by a life-shaping choice, there are multiple admissible answers that are each supportable by good reasons. This does not logically preclude the possibility that for each person there is a singularly best answer to each of the questions. But if this "best" is to be criterial and not arbitrary, the criteria cannot be the same as those that distinguish admissible answers, for those belong to the epistemic condition of multiplism.

Teleology Versus Social Constructionism

An independent source of criteria is provided by the teleological conception of human beings. In this conception, the ideal outcome of each life is within it implicitly from the beginning. It was termed one's daimon by the ancient Greeks, one's genius by ancient Romans and such of their successors in this usage as Emerson and Thoreau, and one's *ubermensch* by Nietzsche; but most latter-day teleologists have been content with "potentialities."

To be sure, teleological understanding of human beings is and always has been contentious, and among teleologists it is a long-standing dispute whether the telos is generic, as in Aristotle on the "dominant end" interpretation of his doctrine, or individuated, as may be the case in Aristotle on an "inclusive end" interpretation and is clearly so for Plato, Nietzsche, Emerson, and Thoreau. My intent is to support an individuated teleological account on the ground that it surpasses nonteleological accounts and generic telos accounts in the intelligibility that it lends to human lives and affairs.

At present the most influential conception of personhood is "social constructionism," which holds that the self is entirely the product of the internalization of social influences by the processes of encultura-tion. The idea that the self *begins* as such was the founding precept of the discipline of sociology in the mid-nineteenth century, and sub-sequent research into the formation of the self in childhood has secured this precept beyond argument. What most certainly *is* dis-putable is the contention by sociological determinists and social constructionists alike that human selves are social products without remainder. My contention is that both of these schools depend for their plausibility on disregarding the developmental dynamics of ad-olescence and the emergent autonomy these dynamics express. But first it is necessary to note the distinction between sociological deter-minism and social constructionism.

Sociological determinism holds that the formation of the self oc-curs by internalization of social constructs (prevailing patterns of perception, belief, feeling, and conduct) and is essentially complete in childhood, with persons necessarily living out their thusly con-ferred identities lifelong. This is to say that it denies individual freedom.

Social constructionism agrees that the formation of the self occurs through internalization of social constructs but leaves room for indi-vidual freedom in two interrelated ways. First, it contends that the social roles by which enculturation operates shape lives in a "soft" way that permits movement by individuals among them as well as within them. Second, enculturation does not assign courses of life to individuals, but provides to them an array of socially sanctioned possibilities among which individuals must choose their particular courses of life.

Adolescence refutes sociological determinism by exhibiting an emergent autonomy that is expressed in the ability of the adolescent to call into question any or all of the central features of his or her prior childhood identity while at the same time entertaining alterna-tives to these central features as candidates for transformative self-identification.

Social constructionism can accommodate transformative self-identification as just described, but with two restrictions, namely, that it is confined to possibilities within the socially sanctioned array, and that if self-identification is criterial and not arbitrary, it will be according to socially prevailing criteria that have been emplanted by enculturation, for according to social constructionism there can be no other source.

It is because emergent autonomy is the introduction of a criterion that does not prevail in society that the onset of adolescence is a crisis in the life of the individual of the kind Thoreau refers to when he says, "Our molting season, like that of the fowls, must be a crisis in our lives. The loon retires to solitary ponds to spend it. Thus also the snake casts its slough, and the caterpillar its wormy coat, by an internal industry and expansion."[15] What is being sloughed is the cocoon of conferred childhood identity, and what beckons is the developmental work of self-identification; but in the interim the individual finds himself naked and alone. In the Chinese language, the kanji for "crisis" is represented by two characters, one of which means "danger" and the other "opportunity."

Emerson captures perfectly the conjunction of danger and opportunity in the sensibility of early adolescence: "What good is near you, when you have life in yourself, it is not by any known or accustomed way; you shall not discern the footprints of any other; you shall not see the face of man; you shall not hear any name;—the way, the thought, the good, shall be wholly strange and new."[16]

To cover its nakedness, adolescence hastily cloaks itself in the peer group and adopts ritualized clan behavior; but the clan is a cloak, well-contrived to conceal within its folds an individuation that cannot as yet bear exposure to direct sunlight. In the group, the adolescent knows himself or herself to be not of the group. Behind his resolute conformity he knows himself to be—in the profoundest sense of the word—*unprepared.* Here, I think, is the *internal* origin of shame in human beings. It is the feeling that attends the prospect of being discovered naked, not in body but in spirit.

This phenomenology of early adolescence is quite inexplicable in the terms of social constructionism, according to which the self-identification that succeeds childhood dependence is upon well-trodden paths sanctioned by society.

In the matter of explanatory power, my contention here is that like sociological determinism, social constructionism cannot account for the distinctive dynamics of adolescence. In consequence, it cannot acknowledge adolescence as a distinctive stage of development with its special developmental work to do, namely the work of self-identification that begins in discovery of one's innate potentialities (self-discovery) and extends to progressively increasing self-knowledge interwoven with self-enactment, and is productive in adult life both of objective value and of the satisfaction of self-fulfillment that the Greeks termed *eudaimonia*.

Failure to recognize adolescence as a distinctive stage of development leaves in place its characteristic dynamics. I refer to dynamics that are implicit in the portrait of adolescence as impulsive, rash, insecure, fickle, insolent, proud, clannish, extremist, and self-preoccupied that appears in Homer's depiction of the youthful Achilles, in Aristotle, in Shakespeare, in Robert Louis Stevenson, in Erik Erikson, and in many other perceptive oberservers of the stage. (As thus characterized, adolescence does not appear in tribal and totalitarian societies, but neither does the degree of autonomy and individuation that we expect of adults. My argument is, however, that the worth of autonomy and individuation depends upon soundness in persons' life-shaping choices, for which the distinctive developmental work of adolescence is the necessary preparation.) Because such failure sees no distinctive developmental work to be done by these traits, it regards them as quirks, leading to the judgment of adolescence itself as a temporary aberration in an otherwise sensible life. In this case, we can believe that we are doing adolescence a favor by squeezing it to extinction between prolonged expectations of childhood dependence and premature expectations of the committed living of adulthood.

Totalitarian Implications in Social Constructionism

A second unfortunate consequence of social constructionism is that it has totalitarian implications. To see this we must be able to recognize totalitarianism without its Orwellian trappings. By definition it means total control of individuals by social agencies. When this brings to mind jackboots, informants, and spy cameras, we have not yet arrived at its requisite means. In C. S. Peirce's words, "No institution can undertake to regulate opinions on every subject. Only the most important ones can be attended to, and on the rest men's minds must be left to the action of natural causes."[17] Independent thinking on the periphery of belief will inevitably in the long run make its way to the center.

The truly effective means of totalitarianism is expressed in the motto, "Give us a child until the age of twelve, and he or she will be ours for life." If persons cannot do other than live out their socially constructed identities lifelong, then totalitarianism prevails no matter what the scope of their subsequent choices may be, because the selves that do the choosing are entirely and without remainder social products.

Deliberate totalitarian conditioning eliminates options in two ways. It produces young people who are equipped only for the courses of life they are expected to pursue; and it inculcates the belief that the alternatives are degenerate, perverse, or evil.

Social constructionism produces trace-effects of totalitarianism in our democratic society. For example, when American business management from the 1940s to the mid-1980s sought to justify itself in shaping not only work and the workplace but also the values and the self-identifications of workers, it relied on the argument that since human beings are in any case social products, they might as well be products of the business corporation that employs them. In its more sophisticated forms, this "corporate culture" approach of management sided with social constructionism (and against sociological determinism) in affirming human freedom, but conditioned employees in the presuppositions that would lead them to agree with management directives about how their freedom was to be used.[18] As if in anticipation of this, beginning around 1914 American schools and classrooms had been transformed to "command and control" management in the interest of efficiency at turning out "products for the market." This occurred during the vogue for "scientific management," which was held by its founder, Frederick W. Taylor, to en-

100

hance the productive efficiency of every type of organization. The inefficiency of our public school system by business standards made it an obvious target, and over a decade it was captured by "Taylorism."[19] Again, an important argument was that since young people can be nothing but products of the system without remainder, command and control management blamelessly and responsibly makes the most of necessity. It is deeply ironic that today our public school classrooms still predominantly operate by command and control, as corporate America is struggling to displace it by "participative management" in an organizational restructuring that is deemed necessary to retain or regain competitive positioning in world and domestic markets.

A consequence of the postulate that every human being is the bearer of innate and distinctive potential worth is that it provides justifying reasons in support of Kant's imperative, "Act so that you treat humanity, whether in your own person or in that of another, always as an end and never as a means only."[20] It is a matter of general agreement that Kant's a priorist and deductive proof of the imperative fails; and I have contended that propositions of its type, namely directional propositions, are insusceptible of either empirical or conceptual proof. Kant's imperative is strengthened by the teleological postulate, but the type of justification to which they are together susceptible is pragmatic: acting on them produces better consequences than acting in disregard of them.

Some Educational Implications

Elementary and secondary education is of vital importance in any society because the half-truth in the sociological tenet that human beings are social products is that they are such in their early years. The effect of introducing the teleological postulate and the Kantian imperative that it supports is that educators must respect and enlist the innate incentive to learn and to grow that is conspicuous in children and young people. To do this requires that children's spontaneous interests be accorded a place in their classrooms, and that in regard to subject-matters in which children lack spontaneous inter-

101

est it must be the responsibility of teachers to begin each new study by first provoking in students the questions to which the study is designed to provide answers.[21]

In contrast, the deadening preface, "You will need to know this," is the hallmark of "top down" education that imposes a curriculum to which children's spontaneous interests are declared to be irrelevant. At a stroke, the innate incentive to learn is banished in favor of the manufactured incentives of credits, grades, and diplomas, and "successful" students are those who accede to the transformation of themselves into "classroom products." The result is the systematic extinction in children of the spontaneous motivation upon which depend the processes of self-identification in adolescence and self-directed living in adulthood.

Certainly there are pitfalls to teleologically based education as there are to education of any kind, and Israel Scheffler has identified three. What I will endeavor to show is that they reflect, not teleology itself as Scheffler appears to think, but misconceptions of it, mostly by educators, but some by formulators of teleological theory. Scheffler identifies three pitfalls to which he gives the names, "the myth of fixed potentials," "the myth of harmonius potentials," and "the myth of uniformly valuable potentials."[22]

Strictly construed, "fixed" potentials denote atemporal "essences" whose embodiment in obviously temporal human beings would constitute an irreconcilable dualism.[23] That this is the case with the teleologies of Plato and Aristotle is undeniable, but my intent is to show that such ahistorical essentialism in regard to potentialities is not connected to teleological theory logically and necessarily, but rather historically and contingently. To this purpose I will combine arguments by Michael Krausz and C. I. Lewis.

In an essay entitled "On Being Jewish," Krausz provides the following: "Here we should distinguish essentialism—the doctrine that there are ahistorically fixed conditions for a thing to be that thing—from what, at particular moments in historical evolution, are taken to be necessary conditions for a thing to be that thing. For example, just as requirements for membership in a community may change over time, it remains that at any given time there are requirements for membership."[24]

Lewis says of his "pragmatic a priori" that what it is prior to is present and future experience and time, not the whole of experience and time. To perform its function, the a priori needn't be utterly unchanging; it will provide the requisite stability in human thought if its rate of change is very slow compared to the rapid fluctuations of unmediated or inadequately mediated experience. In Lewis's image, the roller coaster needn't be anchored on solid rock, but only upon a foundation considerably more stable than itself.[25]

Earlier I contended for "problematicity" as atemporally definitive of human beings, but Lewis's image remains apt because it is not problematicity that stabilizes the roller coaster but the humanly devised correctives to problematicity, and as was noted, the correctives are historicized.

Regarding innate potentialities to function as I contend they can and should do, they must be prior to the experience of the individual and not products of it, but it remains entirely possible that they are evolutionary products of human history, in which case we might term them "temporalized essences."[26] Whether temporalized or not, potentialities as "essences" cannot be used a priori to foreclose persons' futures, because what an individual's potentialities are is only discoverable experimentally and a posteriori, and their discovery is not a terminus but the opening of a path of ongoing exploration and discovery.

Scheffler notes that on the notion of fixed potentials, a student's "evident lacks may be routinely taken for permanent educational deficiencies," and the same can undoubtedly occur on the premise of temporalized essences.[27] Where it occurs it represents a failure to recognize that potentialities are latent before they are manifest. Because an evident lack in a student is consistent with absence of the potentiality and with latency, the former conclusion by teachers of the young is never warranted. From this it does not follow that the teleological conception is pedagogically empty. What follows is that education must incorporate what John Gardner calls the "principle of multiple chances" together with Maria Montessori's "readiness" principle.[28]

Possibilities and Potentialities

Scheffler's other two "myths" both arise from failure to recognize in the teleological conception the necessary distinction between "possibilities" and "potentialities." If we grant that for every normal human being countless alternative courses of life are possible but many will not be lived, then we are recognizing that within all persons are countless possibilities that are fated to remain unactualized. What are termed "potentialities" are a set of possibilities that for each person are "weighted" in the sense that actualizing those possibilities provides to the individual the intrinsic satisfaction that the Greeks called *eudaimonia* and defined as the happiness of self-fulfillment. Other possibilities can be actualized; but they are without this intrinsic satisfaction and must find their motivation among such alternatives as material rewards, social approval, power, fame, duty, fear, revenge, and resentment.

Among the possibilities that exist within every person, many would be productive of social value but not of *eudaimonia*; many conflict with one another and, therefore, either are incompossible or introduce crippling contradictions. Possibilities of evil of every sort are included. Accordingly, it is not the case in teleological theory that all possibilities within persons are "harmonious," nor are they "uniformly valuable."

The harmoniousness of the weighted possibilities of each individual that constitute his or her potentialities is established by the self-identity and the objective worth of his or her telos. This means that if what appears to be among the individual's set of potentialities cannot be integrated with his or her other potentialities, or is not contributory to the objective value of the whole, it is not a potentiality but a possibility that has been mistaken for a potentiality. In short, the conditions of integration and of objective worth are included in the meaning of "potentialities." The evidence that this is not mere stipulative definition is that persons in fact find intrinsic satisfaction in the actualization of some possibilities and not others; that the presence of integrity in some persons demonstrates the integratability of potentialities; and that such lives characteristically manifest objective worth.

In sum, from teleological premises it follows that potentialities are "harmonius" and "uniformly valuable" and, hence, susceptible of being integrated into a worthy life. The implausibility that leads Scheffler to apply the term "myth" stems from failure by educators and Scheffler himself to recognize in teleological theory the necessary distinction between potentialities and possibilities.

Evil

To be sure, evil lives are lived, and probably in some cases they are enjoyed. But enjoyment in evil is enjoyment in destruction of good, and this is a perversion of the original and inherent human relationship to the good, which is that of attraction. Plato and Aristotle provide the classical and enduringly best account of the evil that results from misconceptions of the good, and lately John Kekes has provided an insightful account of other forms of inadvertent evil.[29] What remains is the evil will, which I have just defined as the deliberate ambition to destroy goodness. It is rendered intelligible by Nietzsche's *ressentiment* thesis that the original aspiration to the good in every human being, which is exemplified by the innate incentive in children to learn and to grow, can be transformed by obstacles in the world or in the self to a thematic desire to avenge oneself upon real or imagined adversaries, and ultimately to hatred of humankind including self-hatred.[30]

Social Order

Both the presence of evil and the necessity for social order entail the rule of law and the guidance of custom, not, however, as ends in themselves, but as requisite social supports for self-fulfilling lives. The necessary constraints are of two sorts, substantive and procedural. Every society must limit the kinds of lives that are lived within it by limiting the human possibilities whose actualization it endorses. This is largely the function of enculturation, and it must restrict persons' conduct in pursuit of their chosen ends to such means as do not unjustifiably impinge on others' opportunity to similarly conduct themselves. In short, the self-actualization that teleology endorses is a combination of social authority and self-authority, not the abandonment of the former. When such a teleologist as Emerson says, for example, "the only right is what is after my constitution; the only wrong what is against it," he is indulging in an exaggeration for which there is some reason, but one that nevertheless seriously misrepresents teleological theory.[31]

The self-determination that supervenes upon the social determination of the self in the stage of dependence is the interaction of agencies external to the self and agencies within. If the presence of innate potentialities within every person be granted, it remains logically possible that they are not determinate but indeterminate and, therefore, incapable of doing the work that teleology ascribes to them.

In response, I propose that *sufficient* determinateness is attested by the fact that among culturally sanctioned courses of living (vocations, avocations, interpersonal relationships, regional lifestyles, etc.) each individual experiences as intrinsically rewarding only a select and interrelated few. Criterial self-determination does not require more determinateness than this. In John Dewey's words, "the termini of tendencies are bands not lines, and the qualities that characterize them form a spectrum instead of being capable of distribution in separate pigeonholes."[32] For example, a person whose keenest satisfaction lies in nurturing the young can find it in parenting, teaching, counselling, mentoring younger colleagues, and a variety of other courses of living.

Moral Necessity

Teleology serves to explain a feature that is sufficiently present in exemplary lives as to merit attention—the felt sense of moral necessity. I have earlier defined moral necessity as a necessity that is an expression of the will of the individual, as distinguished from metaphysical, logical, and causal necessities in which the will has either no place or no freedom. Moral necessity is expressed in Martin Luther's "Here I stand, I can do no other," and in Socrates's relentless practice of philosophy in Athens though it should cost him his life. It is a particular kind of the "inner necessity" that characteristically attends hatred, rage, fanaticism, the empassioned stage of romantic love, and strong habit. Wassily Kandinsky contends that inner necessity is the guiding principle of great works of art. In his words, "The artist must ignore distinctions between 'recognized' or 'unrecognized' conventions of form, the transitory knowledge and demands of his particular age. He must watch his own inner life and hearken to the demands of inner necessity."[33] Carl Jung is describing the inner necessity in his life and work when he says, "I have had much trouble getting along with my ideas. There was a daimon in me, and in the end its presence proved decisive. It overpowered me, and if I was at times ruthless it was because I was in the grip of the daimon. I could never stop at anything once attained. I had to hasten on, to catch up with my vision. Since my contemporaries, understandably, could not perceive my vision, they saw only a fool rushing ahead."[34] Michael Krausz perceptively recognizes inner necessity in the "movement toward closure of a project" and offers the following example: "It is said that as a child Chopin was difficult to raise in the morning. So his mother would play a 5–7 chord on the piano to cause him to jump out of bed in order to resolve it by playing the tonic chord."[35]

Moral necessity shares with all forms of inner necessity the felt sense of compulsion to do what "must" be done in disregard of options. It is distinguished from other forms by its objective dimension, which is the ambition to actualize objective value, that is, value that can be appreciated and utilized by such persons as possess the developed capacities to recognize and utilize value of the particular kind that the given individual aims at actualizing.

I have elsewhere described the subjective dimension of moral necessity as the inseparable conjunction of the feeling of "being where one wants to be, doing what one wants to do," and the feeling of "being where one must be, doing what one must do."[36] It is conceivable, of course, that the prospect for arrving at it is limited to a small percentage of the human populace that is exceptionally favored by the "natural lottery of birth"; but there are good reasons for the alternative supposition that the conditions of moral necessity are in principle accessible to all human beings. In the first place, as Abraham Maslow found in his studies of self-actualizing human beings, the sense of moral necessity is a shared characteristic; second, if innate potentialities are an inseparable part of what it is to be a human being, then both self-actualization and moral necessity are in principle open to all persons. Summarizing his research among self-actualizing persons, Maslow says,

> In the ideal instance, which fortunately also happens in fact in many of my instances, "I want to" coincides with "I must." There is a good matching of inner with outer requiredness. And the observer is then over-awed by the degree of compellingness, of inexorability, of preordained destiny, necessity, and harmony that he perceives. Furthermore, the observer (as well as the person involved) feels not only that "it has to be" but also that "it ought to be, it is right, it is suitable, appropriate, fitting, and proper."[37]

Second, universality of the prospect for moral necessity is supported by the ontology of human being as problematic being. If, as I have contended, to be a human being is to be first of all a problem to oneself, this is because human beings lack the fixity that characterizes every other form of being by virtue of ontological necessity. This is humankind's freedom and also its predicament. Not only must human beings decide what to become and endeavor to become it, but in order to lead effective lives they must equip themselves with a substitute for the ontological necessity that they lack, and the substitute must be compatible with human freedom. This substitute is moral necessity.

We may speak, then, of the *necessity* of moral necessity in well-lived lives, and Henry Thoreau implies it by his description of lives in which moral necessity is lacking: "It is remarkable that there are few men so well employed, so much to their minds, but that a little money or fame would commonly buy them off from their present pursuit."[38] In a moment, I will show that moral necessity is clearly distinguishable from the fanaticism that is an outgrowth of dogmatic absolutism.

A problem with multiplism in the absence of moral necessity is that it can too readily become a fair weather philosophy. If the good reasons that connect a person to his or her values are matched by equally good reasons in support of his or her connection to alternative values, then when the person's professed values are threatened or require arduous effort in their behalf, he or she can with impunity shift allegiance to a different set and repeat the process when new difficulties arise.

In this connection, it is important to recognize that teleological theory is not hedonistic, for if it were hedonistic then the inevitable pains that attend the actualization, conservation, and defense of one's values would justify a shift to other values, and so on endlessly. But teleology entails a distinction between two different categories of pains. For each person there are pains that have no inherent connection to his or her best course of living, and others that are integral to it. Pains of the first sort are to be avoided insofar as possible. Pains of the second sort cannot be avoided without failure in self-responsibility. Moreover they participate in the distinctive kind of satisfaction or happiness that attends self-fulfilling living, and we do not misstate the case to term them "welcome pains."

The developmental importance of welcome pains is nowhere clearer than in adolescence, which notoriously seeks out painful experiences for what adults perceive as no sensible reason. In fact, they provide the adolescent with reassurance that he or she is living authentically, having emerged from the protective clearing of childhood. At this juncture, pain is privileged evidence, because it was in good part for protection from pain that the individual's childhood was supervised by adults. Because childhood is to be outgrown, there is good developmental reason for an adolescent to savor the physical pain, say, of grueling running, or the fear of a cliff dive; and reassurance is typically enhanced by the added pain of parental disapproval of the particular activity. The same applies to the adolescent who appears to wallow in the anguish of a broken romance, when adults know that another romance will soon follow.

"Rootless Cosmopolitanism"

Moral necessity has direct bearing on the present contention by com-
munitarians and traditionalists that personal choice is an unreliable
basis for commitment. According to Alasdair MacIntyre, for example,
basing allegiances upon personal choice has led to today's "rootless
cosmopolitanism" of persons who "temporarily adopt the standpoint
of a tradition and then exchange it for another, as one might first
wear one costume and then another, or as one might act one part in
one play and then a quite different part in a quite different play."[39]

In *Habits of the Heart*, Robert Bellah and coauthors provide the
following characterization of twentieth-century American "individualism": "No binding obligations and no wider social understanding
justify a relationship. It exists only as the expression of the choices of
the free selves who make it up. And should these no longer meet
their needs, it must end." As does MacIntyre, these authors attribute
our weakening ties of kinship, religious fellowship, and civic friend-
ship to the liberal endeavor to found them upon choice, and com-
mend instead relations that are "independent of the individual's will
and can to a considerable extent be taken for granted."[40] F. A.
Hayek drives traditionalism's point home by contending that "Principles are often effective guides for action when they appear as no
more than an unreasoned prejudice, a general feeling that certain
things simply 'are not done'; while as soon as they are explicitly
stated speculation begins about their correctness and their validity."[41]

In diametrical opposition to the direction indicated by MacIntyre,
Bellah et al., and Hayek, I contend that we must look to a necessity
in human lives that issues *from the furtherance of human freedom
and reflective awareness*, and not from their relinquishment. It may
be the case that most of what passes among us as "commitments"
are unworthy of the name. My argument is that the direction in
which to look for the corrective is not that of the curtailment of
choice in an unquestioning subservience to received tradition, but to
the generalized opportunity for individuals to discover chosen
courses of life that actualize their innate potentialities and are
thereby invested with moral necessity.

Traditionalism's case against choice relies for its persuasiveness upon disregarding a distinction that few of us fail to make in our daily lives, namely the distinction between "choices" and choices. Some "choices" are made by persons who have no intention of being bound by their entailments (for example, a man who marries while secretly reserving to himself some of the prerogatives of bachelorhood). Some "choices" are made with almost no effective knowledge of alternatives (exemplified in vocational "choices" made by young people whose experience is entirely circumscribed by classroom, household, peer group, and homogeneous neighborhood). Some "choices" are made by people who, as we say, "don't know their own minds."

It will be evident that the attribution of rootless dilettantism to chosen association is simplistic if we remind ourselves of some of history's instances of chosen commitments that were lived out unwaveringly, among them the cases of Luther and Socrates that were mentioned before; the conversions of St. Paul and St. Augustine to Christianity; the conversion of Cardinal Newman to Roman Catholicism; the commitment of Heloise and Abelard to one another; and the commitments to our country of countless immigrants. It will also be evident from such examples that one's chosen course of life is not traditionless, for the effect of choice is to exchange received tradition for chosen tradition, namely the tradition that is represented by one's predecessors in the chosen course. To the cynical argument that only perfection deserves total commitment and nothing that is humanly experienceable or conceivable qualifies, the appropriate rejoinder is "Fortunately so; for perfection renders human commitment gratuitous."

Fanaticism

The familiar contention that moral necessity is indistinguishable from fanaticism is erroneous. The crucial distinction is that fanaticism is ready to impose its own ideals upon unconsenting others, while moral necessity, to be "moral," *presupposes multiplism* because it recognizes choice; and to recognize the freedom and self-

111

responsibility that choice implies, it must honor the condition of consent. In Thoreau's words, "I would not have anyone adopt *my* mode of living on any account; for, besides that before he has fairly learned it I may have found out another for myself, I desire that there may be as many different persons in the world as possible; but I would have each one be very careful to find out and pursue his own way, and not his father's or his mother's or his neighbor's instead."[42]

Moral necessity is the postreflective counterpart to the pre-reflective commitment in the "innocent parochialism-to-dogmatic absolutism-to-fanaticism" progression. The intervening recognition is the epistemic multiplism of the "directional" propositions that by the argument of this chapter are indispensable to human lives as answers to the problematicity of human being.

Self-knowledge

Central to well-lived lives on a teleological account is knowledge of one's innate potentialities, which is self-knowledge. It is unsurprising if moral necessity is rare among us, for nothing in our established patterns of education and the rearing of our young is directed to their acquisition of self-knowledge. This is our heritage from modernity's renunciation of teleology, together with its early disjunctive conceptions of "objectivity" and "subjectivity" in knowledge. Relegation of self-knowledge to the side of the subjectivism that is thought to contaminate objectivity has resulted in a general discrediting of the enterprise of self-knowledge as idle self-indulgence if not the pathology of narcissism.[43] The disjunctive conceptions of objectivity and subjectivity were decisively overturned by Immanuel Kant and are no longer operative in the sciences. But in the absence of a teleological conception of human beings, self-knowledge has no function and is accorded no place in our patterns of education.

To fail to cultivate self-knowledge in young people is to fail to provide them with one of the two conditions for soundness in their life-shaping choices. The other condition for soundness is adequate working knowledge of the alternatives in regard to each of the life-shaping choices, and our failure to recognize adolescence as a dis-

112

tinctive stage of development with its distinctive developmental work to do is our failure to equip young people with this second condition. Instead of taking adolescence's inherent adventurousness—its compulsion to leap the fences that marked off its prior childhood as a protected clearing—as our cue to its developmental work, and facilitating it, we equate it with irresponsibility and consider that we are saving adolescence from itself by our unrelieved imposition of command and control schooling.[44]

Adolescence and Liberality

Facilitated exploration in adolescence is the breeding ground of the virtue of liberality because, as was noted in chapter 1, adolescence explores possibilities by participatory enactment, perpetually posing to itself the question, "What would it be like to be this other, that other?," and so on. Participatory enactment discloses truths and values in alternative courses of life. Then when one in due course answers for oneself the directional question, "Which truths and values shall I be responsible for?," one is positioned to acknowledge the validity of alternative courses of life whose truths and values are comparably the responsibility of other persons.

I have identified adolescence with the adventure of exploration, but any well-lived adulthood also includes exploration. The difference is that the exploration of adolescence is among possibilities regarded as candidates for eventual commitment, while adult exploration is primarily within the various strands of the individual's chosen course of life. But, alike, the quality of one's relations with others and the soundness of one's self-knowledge require exercise in adulthood of the imaginative capacity for participatory enactment that a well-lived adolescence cultivates.

Beyond Tolerance

The case is analogous for each determinate culture in our multicultural world. Not insularity but cooperative interaction is mandated by the global scope of exigent human problems, and such cooperative interaction can only be stabilized by the readiness and the ability of each nation and culture to substantively (not merely formally) recognize the worth of the distinctive contributions of other nations and cultures. This is the virtue of liberality in its cross-cultural expression, and I will conclude by contrasting it with classical liberalism's celebrated virtue of "tolerance." The difference to which I want to call attention appears in Michael Krausz's comparison of the self-interpretations of Clifford Geertz and Richard Rorty, and I will begin with it.

Krausz says, "Geertz's self-characterization as white, male, bourgeois, intellectual, and so on, resembles Rorty's self-characterization. But such a self-characterization is for Geertz *initial*, while for Rorty it is *final* in the sense that Rorty seems to see no need for self-development through confrontation with alternative cultures. Put otherwise, Geertz's ethnocentrism encourages a development in inquirers, while Rorty's does not."[45]

Rorty faultlessly exemplifies the classical liberal virtue of tolerance, and he also illustrates its deficiency. Certainly tolerance is a great advance over dogmatic absolutism's intolerance because it is a peaceable accommodation of diversity. Its defect is that tolerance can be fully expressed by ignoring others. On the world scene, the old American isolationism is consistent with toleration of others; but ignoring others is no longer possible when besetting human problems are global in scope and will require interactive cooperation if they are to be promisingly addressed. Such cooperation can only be stabilized by the recognition of varieties of truth and value and the distributed responsibility among alternative cultures for realization and harmonization of this variety. This is a multiplist recognition that is inconsistent with the insularity of liberalism's "live and let live" and liberalism's underlying presuppositions of atomistic individuality and absolute national sovereignty.

To be sure, liberalism's "perimeter of protective rights" remains necessary to preserve the autonomy of cooperating entities, but the meaning of "autonomy" changes. Its meaning under classical liberalism idealizes the presupposed atomicity of protected entities as "total self-sufficiency." In order to commensurate "autonomy" with

114

the inherent interdependence of entities that are participants in a division of labor with respect to the realization of truth and value, I propose as its meaning: the entitlement of each interactive entity to determine for itself what its contributions to others will be and, likewise, to determine for itself what use it will make of the self-determined contributions of other entities.

Notes

1. Ideals of "complete humanness" vary from culture to culture but cannot be lacking in any culture by virtue of the inevitable role of culture in preparing successive generations of children and young people for adult life by the processes we term "socialization" and "enculturation." To do this requires a guiding ideal of fully functional adulthood. Beneath cultural variability undoubtedly may be found some common characteristics in ideals of full humanness—some basic physical, cognitive, and affective capacities. But by our argument of chapter 1, this cannot serve as a "common ground" upon which to build an interpretive framework that is uniform across all cultures, because the variables in every culture's conception of full humanness determine the meanings for that culture of the universals. In short, by "ideals of full humanness" I am not here introducing a decontextualized criterion.

2. Michael Krausz, *Rightness and Reasons: Interpretation in Cultural Practices* (Ithaca: Cornell University Press, 1993), p. 4.

3. Ibid., p. 166.

4. Ibid., pp. 105–6. For Krausz's summary on multiplism see pp. 44–45.

5. Ibid., pp. 21–22.

6. Ibid., p. 51.

7. Ibid., pp. 22–32.

8. Illustrative is Krausz's argument against the purported neutrality of Charles Taylor's "language of perspicuous contrast." See Krausz, *Rightness and Reasons*, pp. 107–9.

9. Krausz, *Rightness and Reasons*, p. 17.

10. Ibid.; Chapters 3 and 4 treat the issue of imputationalism vs. anti-imputationalism in interpretation, and chapters 6 and 7 treat ontological realism versus ontological constructionalism.

11. Ibid., p. 166.

12. Cited in Krausz, *Rightness and Reasons*, p. 135.

13. Karl Popper, "Truth and Approximation to Truth," in *Popper Selec-*

tions, ed. David Miller (Princeton: Princeton University Press, 1985), p. 185. Hilary Putnam, *Reason, Truth, and History* (Cambridge: Cambridge University Press, 1981), notably the final sentence of the book: "The very fact that we speak of our different conceptions of *rationality* posits a *Grenzbegriff*, a limit-concept of the ideal truth." Putnam's "internal realism" is avowedly pluralistic, beginning in "moral images of the world," which according to Putnam are irreducibly multiple (*The Many Faces of Realism*, p. 86) and which condition "fact" through the indispensable notion of "relevance" (*Reason, Truth, and History*, pp. 201–2), and are homes to alternative forms of life. But for this plurality to be irreducibly such, there must be irreducibly multiple "limit concepts of the ideal truth."

14. Krausz, *Rightness and Reasons*, p. 43.

15. Henry D. Thoreau, *Walden*, ed. J. Lyndon Shanley (Princeton: Princeton University Press, 1971), p. 24.

16. Ralph Waldo Emerson, "Self-Reliance," *The Collected Works of Ralph Waldo Emerson* (Cambridge: Harvard University Press, 1979), vol. 2, p. 39.

17. Charles S. Peirce, "The Fixation of Belief," in *Selected Writings*, ed. Philip P. Weiner (New York: Dover, 1966), p. 105.

18. See, e.g., William G. Scott, *Chester I. Bernard and the Guardians of the Managerial State* (Lawrence: University Press of Kansas, 1992), esp. ch. 7. In another place, Scott shows that the combined work of Barnard and Simon brought orthodox management theory, around 1950, "as close as it had [come] before or has since to a legitimate paradigm of thought." The paradigm included shaping workers' presuppositions so as to secure agreement with management decisions. See Scott, "The Concentric Circles of Management Thought," in *Papers in the Ethics of Administration*, ed. N. Dale Wright (Albany: State University of New York Press, 1988), p. 28.

19. Extensive documentation is collated in Raymond E. Callahan, *Education and the Cult of Efficiency* (Chicago: University of Chicago Press, 1962).

20. Immanuel Kant, *Foundations of the Metaphysics of Morals*, trans. Lewis White Beck (Indianapolis: Bobbs-Merrill Library of Liberal Arts, 1959), p. 47.

21. I have spelled out educational implications in more detail in David L. Norton, "Education for Self-Knowledge and Worthy Living," in *Ethical Issues in Contemporary Society*, ed. John Howie and George Schedler (Carbondale: Southern Illinois University Press, 1994), chap. 6.

22. Israel Scheffler, *Of Human Potential: An Essay in the Philosophy of Education* (Boston, London: Routledge & Kegan Paul, 1985), pp. 10–16.

23. As noted earlier, irreconcilable (disjunctive) dualism is not entailed by my claim in behalf of the "essential" problematicity of being human. As a lack that calls for remedy, problematicity entails history as the arena in which solutions are necessarily to be sought.

24. Michael Krausz, "On Being Jewish," in *Jewish Identity*, ed. David Theo Goldberg and Michael Krausz (Philadelphia: Temple University Press, 1993), p. 267.

25. Clarence Irving Lewis, *Mind and the World Order* (New York: Dover, 1956), p. 138.

26. The term was suggested by Michael Krausz in conversation.

27. Scheffler, *Of Human Potential*, p. 11.

28. John W. Gardner, *Excellence* (New York: Harper & Row Perennial Library, 1971), p. 80.

29. John Kekes, *Facing Evil* (Princeton: Princeton University Press, 1990). Kekes focuses on unintentional evil, which he argues is evil's predominant form.

30. Friedrich Nietzsche, *On the Genealogy of Morals*, trans. Walter Kaufmann (New York: Random House Vintage Books, 1969). Nietzsche's discussion of *ressentiment* is distributed through Essays 1 and 2.

31. Ralph Waldo Emerson, "Self Reliance," *Collected Works*, vol. 2, p. 30.

32. John Dewey, *Art as Experience* (New York: G. P. Putnam's Capricorn Books, 1958), p. 224.

33. Wassily Kandinsky, *Concerning the Spiritual in Art* (New York: Wittenborn, Schulz, Inc., 1947), p. 53. I owe this reference to Michael Krausz.

34. Carl G. Jung, *Memories, Dreams, Reflections*, ed. Aniela Jaffe, trans. Richard and Clara Winston, rev. ed. (New York: Pantheon Books, 1973), p. 356.

35. Michael Krausz, preliminary draft dated 7/3/94 for a work in progress tentatively entitled *Culture and Interpretation*.

36. David L. Norton, *Personal Destinies* (Princeton: Princeton University Press, 1976), p. 222.

37. Abraham H. Maslow, "A Theory of Metamotivation: The Biological Rooting of the Value-Life," *Journal of Humanistic Psychology*, 7, no. 2 (fall 1967): 96.

38. Henry D. Thoreau, "Life without Principle," in Thoreau, *Reform Papers*, ed. Wendell Glick (Princeton: Princeton University Press, 1973), p. 159.

39. Alasdair MacIntyre, *Whose Justice? Which Rationality?* (Notre Dame: University of Notre Dame Press, 1988), p. 367.

40. Robert N. Bellah, Richard Madsen, William M. Sullivan, Ann Swindler, Steven M. Tipton, *Habits of the Heart: Individualism and Commitment in American Life* (Berkeley, Los Angeles: University of California Press, 1985), p. 114.

41. Friedrich A. Hayek, *Law, Legislation, and Liberty* (Chicago: University of Chicago Press, 1973), vol. 1, p. 60.

42. Thoreau, *Walden*, p. 71.

43. A detailed history of these ideas is provided in my *Democracy and Moral Development* (Berkeley, Los Angeles: University of California Press, 1991), chap. 2.

44. It is possibilities *in the world* to which adolescent exploration is attracted, and to facilitate adolescent exploration requires combining classroom learning with practical experience, for example, by work-study programs and a national youth service. I develop these implications in my *Democracy and Moral Development*, chap. 3, "Implementation of Developmental Democracy: Focus Upon Adolescence."

45. Krausz, *Rightness and Reasons*, p. 113.

INDEX

ABOUT THE AUTHOR

David L. Norton, for thirty years a member of the Department of Philosophy at the University of Delaware, received his Ph.D. from Boston University. He published almost a hundred articles and reviews in philosophical journals, popular magazines, and books of collected essays. His books include *Personal Destinies* (1976) and *Democracy and Moral Development* (1991), as well as a volume co-edited with his wife, Mary K. Norton, *Philosophies of Love* (Littlefield Adams Quality Paperbacks, 1994). Professor Norton received an honorary doctorate from Soka University in Japan, and published a short book, *Japanese Buddhism and the American Renaissance,* in separate Japanese and English versions in 1993.

David Norton died of cancer, unexpectedly and after a brief illness, in July 1995.